No Pain, No Gain

No Pain, No Gain

HOPE FOR THOSE WHO STRUGGLE

JOHN R. WIMMER

CARMEL · NEW YORK 10512

A Ballantine/Epiphany Book

This Guideposts edition is published by
special arrangement with Ballantine Books.

Library of Congress Cataloging in Publication Data

Wimmer, John R., 1956–
    No pain, no gain.

    Includes bibliographical references.
    1. Christian life—Methodist authors. 2. Suffering—
Religious aspects—Christianity. 3. Theodicy. I. Title.
BV4501.2.W564   1985   248.4'87606   84–24241

Manufactured in the United States of America
Text design by Holly Johnson

First Edition: November 1985

10 9 8 7 6 5 4 3 2

For, and with, Jan

There is a curious paradox
That no one can explain.
Who understands the secret
Of the reaping of the grain?

Who understands why Spring is born
Out of Winter's laboring pain?
Or why we all must die a bit
Before we grow again.

—*The Fantasticks*

CONTENTS

ACKNOWLEDGMENTS

This is the most difficult page of this book to write, for there are many more persons who deserve thanks than can be mentioned here. To all these people whose support is so valued, I can only hope to express gratitude in other significant ways. Among these there are a few whom I especially wish to acknowledge.

First I want to thank my spouse, Jan Blaising, for her insights, her creativity, and her integrity, which have influenced this book beyond what words can adequately express. In fact, we have spent so many hours together sharing and talking about these matters that the difference between her thoughts and mine expressed here are virtually indistinguishable. The hours we share together make me more thankful each day she is the one with whom I share life.

Our families, Wimmers and Blaisings, deserve thanks for their seemingly endless patience and loving support that has meant so much for many years.

Also I express my gratitude to Adolf Hansen (whose unique ability to combine spirituality and scholarship has influenced me greatly), Rob Rollins, John VanVactor, Jack Pavy, Brian Witwer, and the Wednesday A.M. Study Group at First United Methodist Church in West Lafayette, Indiana, for their ideas, friendship, and caring. Special appreciation also belongs to Michelle Rapkin of Ballantine Books for her wise and gracious editorial guidance, as well as to Marjorie Braman and Toni Simmons.

INTRODUCTION

Perhaps no one really knows who coined the phrase "no pain, no gain," although it sounds like something the ever-winning Green Bay Packers coach Vince Lombardi would have said.

The idea is not only basic vocabulary for striving athletes but can be employed by struggling Christians as well.

I vividly recall the first time I heard the words. Having faced the fact that I needed to lose weight, I'd begun a regimen of dieting and daily jogging. So proud was I of my progress that one evening I decided to show off my achievement: I invited a friend to run with me. I didn't know he was in much better physical condition than I. By the time we had run two-and-a-half miles (already half a mile more than I usually ran by myself), discomfort overcame pride and I begged my friend to stop our running. I gasped out the news that my lungs ached and my legs felt as if they would soon fall off! "Come on, John!" came the response. "*No pain, no gain!*"

Wise coaches place that maxim on bulletin boards and posters in weight-workout rooms and athletic locker rooms; they know their would-be disciples need encouraging reminders that athletic excellence has a price tag.

"No pain, no gain" implies that in order for you to be a good athlete, for you to become a true champion, you must be willing to persevere through the pain. Your efforts will cost you; you must extend yourself to the very edge of your endurance—to the point where you experience pain. Yet beyond that threshold lie greater endurance, confidence, and ability than if this pain and gain is not encountered.

As my friend urged me on that evening while we ran, I certainly felt intense pain. Yet his words reminded me of the progress I'd already made in both dieting and distance running. At first I had lost very little weight and was capable of running only half a mile. But soon, and with no great difficulty, I could run three-fourths of a mile and then a mile. Through my steady exercise and substantial reductions in caloric intake, pounds gradually but consistently melted away. As my mind wandered on these thoughts, and I continued forcing one foot in front of the other, somehow my physical pain seemed a little less intense. And with the first stirrings of faith in those encouraging words "no pain, no gain," I was able to summon the courage to run still farther. That night I experienced the thrill of running past the three-mile marker for the first time.

Then I collapsed!

Nevertheless, even as I was catching my breath and rubbing my sore legs, I knew pleasure, even joy I would not have known had I quit earlier.

I've learned a couple of things since that day I jogged with my friend. One of them is that if I quit jogging, I'd gain thirty pounds—no pain, plenty of gained weight! I also reflected that "no pain, no gain" is not only an athletic principle. Skilled musicians, physicians, business persons, academicians, artists—people in these and other walks of life know that the pain resulting from the struggle of study and practice grows into greater levels of proficiency, healing, and growth. We discover deeper-lying planes of unexplored territory outside us and unrealized creativity within.

Yet, I believe that "no pain, no gain" expresses an even more profound *spiritual* principle. It is one of the basic laws of the universe God is creating; it is a central reality of the Christian faith, in which we suffer, learn, grow, and rejoice. For just like the athlete, a Christian grows in spiritual strength and stamina from having experienced and worked through painful struggles.

That's the opposite of what we are sometimes told Christians ought to be like. We may wrongly assume that as Christians, we should not have any problems—and if we do, it is because we lack faith. Worse still, when we experience spiritual and emotional struggle, too often we are made to feel that we are being punished by God for some sin or wrongful deed we have committed or some good deed neglected. Because we hurt and believe God may be responsible, we naturally feel like angrily shouting at God, "Why are you doing this to me?!" Immediately we are filled with remorse for worsening our unknown sin by shouting at the Creator! We then have no choice but to give up the hope that God will help; to ponder the mystery of our eternal fate as we seethe with pain, loneliness, and anger.

Why do we feel pain in our struggles? Why must we continue to deal with those people and situations that produce suffering? Where is God when we feel this pain?

Questions directed toward God about the nature of life are as old as the stories we read in the accounts of the wandering Israelites questioning God's care as they searched for the Promised Land (Numbers 13–14) or the exiled people bewailing God's absence as they felt the pain of separation from Jerusalem's Temple during their captivity in Babylon (Jeremiah and Lamentations). And there are no easy answers to such searching questions. In the New Testament, probably the most significant question ever asked, the one still echoing through the heavens into our hearts, was uttered by Jesus himself, when he cried from the pain and agony of the cross, "My God, my God, why hast thou forsaken me?" (Matt. 27:46).

As these passages from the Bible show us, in the midst of the pain and suffering we experience in our lives, we must not only cope with the pain itself, but also wrestle with the burden of trying to understand why we must face such painful trials to begin with.

We will not attempt here to answer the rhetorical question of why suffering and evil exist in the world (although we will acknowledge and discuss it). Rather, we will try to understand as best we can what progress is being made by applying the "no pain, no gain" principle in our spiritual life as we engage in struggles. We cannot always understand or control many of the things that happen to us, but we can play a major role in determining our *response* to the struggles we experience. So it is to this response that we will turn most of our attention.

That focus may or may not help banish the pain we face; yet we may begin to understand more fully that every struggle confronting us is an opportunity for spiritual growth. If we make the decision to seize this opportunity for growth, we will indeed experience newer, deeper, more meaningful dimensions of the life God graciously gives us in abundance.

Therefore, to those running "the race that is set before us" (Heb. 12:1) whose lungs ache and whose legs feel as if they will soon fall off—let us discover that gain will come from our pain!

Part I: PAIN

They have an inadequate view of suffering.
—Helmut Thielicke describing the
greatest defect among
American Christians

Our "Painless" Society

Pain hurts!

It seems silly to say something so obvious. Yet this simple statement is one of the hardest lessons we must learn in life. Because we have "an inadequate view of suffering," we act as if pain does not hurt. Many of us try desperately, some of us all of our lives, to deny that pain is a fact of life.

I was both amused and saddened by a story recently told to me by my sister and her husband just before they were blessed with the birth of their first child, Ryan. Like most other couples having children, they were in the process of deciding which method of labor assistance they would use at the time of birth. In enumerating the benefits and shortcomings she had experienced in using one particular method, a friend of my sister's warned her, "There's one major flaw in that program: No one told me that having the baby was going to *hurt!*"

Seldom do people tell us that certain aspects of living are going to be painful. Growing into adulthood—a process that never ceases—presents struggles common to us all but experienced differently by each of us. As some feel the joyous pain of childbirth, others nurse the hurt of infertility. Youthful friendships and peer pressures, dating and breaking up, schoolwork and vocational decisions all have certain growing pains associated with them. Yet adulthood brings its own trying "passages" involving occupational stresses, or unemployment, marriage/family issues, the loss of loved ones, serious illness, midlife crises, aging parents, accidents, retirement, and a host of other stresses provoked by everyday living!

In the face of this reality, our culture tries in countless ways to inform us as we mature from childhood into adulthood that life ought to remain a painless activity. From the time we are infants, it seems, we are soothed and shielded from the discomforts of life. We are pampered with cottony soft diapers, baby powder, and extra-gentle shampoo. Loving us, our parents attempt to smile away the little hurts we encounter. We are cuddled when we cry, fed when hungry, and sometimes spoiled with attention by relatives and friends who love cute little babies.

Love and attention are great! Embracing love and gentle care shown to us as infants and toddlers instills within us an invaluable gift: the message that we are loved and lovable. Yet even with the best love and care (and the most ambitious attempts at spoiling us by proud parents and gift-bearing grandparents), we cannot help but occasionally develop a painful diaper rash! More painfully, some of us, as children, don't receive the care we need and deserve.

As we grow older, we may spend much time and money protecting ourselves from hurt, just as others sheltered us as children. We rely on aspirin to relieve our stress-induced headaches, relaxants to ease overworked muscles, antacids to soothe overworked stomachs. Yet is the upset stomach our real problem or a symptom of a deeper malaise?

Consciously or unconsciously, we experience some pain almost daily resulting from interactions with other people. At work, home, or school, our days include an emotional mixture of such ingredients as frustration, pressure, and competition. And beyond day-to-day discomforts are the more severe physical and emotional disturbances we inevitably face. Tragedies may precipitate deeply trying times, forcing upon us unpleasant facts of life we would rather avoid. A changing economy and cultural expectations may place new pressures on marriages, engagements, parent–child relations, vocational plans. The struggle resulting from such stress may often produce painful decisions that may result in marital or family separations, divorce, career changes, moving, or some other action entailing personal sacrifices. Ours is *not* a painless society!

Wrestling with difficult decisions, we find that living hurts, and we are tempted to seek ways to escape our struggle. In extreme cases we may try to dull the ache through the use and abuse of alcohol or drugs. After all, anyone who has ever sat in front of a TV set knows that quickly ridding ourselves of discomfort is simple and, of course, always desirable: We have only to buy the more powerful antacid, the painkiller that gets into the blood faster to fight our headache, the hemorrhoid ointment that will let us sit more comfortably in our easy chair. Advertisers pay out huge sums in promoting the idea that for a small price we can live in a painless environment.

In such a climate, if we find that our marriage involves more struggle than we had anticipated, divorce or separation can seem to be an easy solution to the immediate pain. In other cases, avoiding difficult marital or other family problems may be a method of evading or postponing terrible hurts. Even if we avoid these more extreme reactions to pain, we may construct imaginary walls around our inner emotional selves, thinking we can be insulated from truly feeling pain.

Some persons even look to the church, or religion, as a monastery to which they can flee the discomfort of the "real world" by cloaking themselves within seemingly religious responses to pain. Yet this use of an escapist "faith" is no better than others' use of alcohol or drugs.

Sometimes an escape into church is valid; it may provide a place where we can, temporarily, leave the trials of daily living behind; where we may find an answer to a specific problem; or where we may find closer communication with

God. This differs greatly from the extremist reaction of "escaping" permanently into the church in order to hide from "real life." Faith should not be used as a method of escape!

After the fleeting numbness has faded from these attempted escapes, we learn that the struggles and sore spots have never really gone away; and in company with this realization, our struggles revisit us at an even more oppressive level of intensity.

Embracing Pain

Given our "inadequate view of suffering," it is no wonder we find it difficult to face our struggles. Yet before we are able to experience the relief, gain, and growth from the pain struggle produces, we must first come face-to-face with the fact that if we want to feel the gain we must first feel the pain.

But it's important to remember that there are two kinds of sufferers. Some people—athletes, for example—willingly take on pain for the specific purpose of self-improvement. Others do not ask for pain yet must experience it no matter how unwillingly.

Ralph Sockman, in his book *The Meaning of Suffering*, points out that some types of pain are perceived as pleasurable. Of course, one's tolerance for self-chosen pain must be very high. Sockman tells of an encounter with a football coach who stated that one of the prime qualifications for a top-notch player is that "he must *enjoy* pain."

We can afford to "enjoy" pain when we voluntarily assume the pain of physical conditioning for the pleasure of sport; or when we choose to take on the emotional struggle of therapy for the pleasure of personal growth; or when we accept the sacrifices of dieting in order to enjoy losing weight! When one chooses pain, the person may realize from the very beginning certain sacrifices must be made in order for the desired gains in strength or growth to be achieved.

But what about the pain we do not inflict upon ourselves? Are those who do not choose their pain supposed to enjoy it as the coach said a good player should?

There are—and should be—definite differences in attitude and motivation between those who willingly encounter pain and those who are forced to deal with intense pain due to mistakes, accidents, illnesses, death, or the not-so-mere everyday tasks that pile up and leave us feeling victimized by life. Although we rarely want to, if we are to enjoy the benefit of gains in our emotional/spiritual life, *we must face our struggle and embrace our pain!* Or as W. C. Fields put it: "There comes a time in the affairs of humanity when you must take the bull by the tail and face the situation!"

At the prospect of thoroughly unpleasant situations, we may think it easier to deal with our problems by simply ignoring them—maybe they'll go away. As we have seen, we may also try to elude the problem by numbing the hurt. The truth is that such avoidance is like sweeping dirt under the carpet: Barring great good luck or a miracle, the problem is still there; it's only temporarily out of sight. And in choosing *not* to deal with pain, we usually find that not only does the hurt fail to go away, it also transfers itself into other areas of our lives.

When I first met Clifford, an elderly man I once knew, I did not like his sour personality; he seemed to lash out at nearly everyone he met. He was grumpy and short-tempered; he complained constantly—and he bitterly described as "stupid" nearly everything anyone did in his presence. I found out later from others who knew him well that he had not been that way before "the accident." A few years before, Clifford's only daughter had been killed in a car crash due to her own negligence in failing to take certain precautionary measures.

I remember the day Clifford first told me about his daughter's death. He began telling the story calmly, but became progressively more angry, finally reaching a climax of rage. He thrust his face at mine, shouting at me how "stupid" it was of his daughter to be so unconcerned with her own safety.

I recognized that tone of voice: The "stupid" sounded exactly like the "stupid" he so habitually applied to others in his dealings with them. When I commented that he seemed angry about his daughter's accident (hoping this would help Clifford draw out his anger), he quickly "got hold of himself" and almost immediately returned to a fake calmness. It seemed as if nothing had happened as he concluded tersely, "I'm not angry. It doesn't matter. It's over now."

But it *wasn't* over, and it *did* matter; he was angry and hurt and had not embraced those feelings in order to express them fully and honestly and let the healing begin. How tragic it was that to the end of his life he displayed the effects of deep pain while refusing to admit to harboring any feelings at all! Consequently, when I met Clifford five years after the tragic death of his daughter, this man who so desperately needed the love and care of other people to help heal his deep pain was repelling all who would offer their concern because his own inability to embrace his pain produced a very unattractive anger at others.

The primary key to embracing pain is to be *honest* about what is hurting us. But it is not always easy to identify the sources of our pain. Of course, when we experience such tragedy as the death of a loved one, most of us find it all too easy to determine the source of our grief; yet sometimes our hurts are disguised by very deeply ingrained avoidance techniques we have acquired or cultivated over years. Maybe we are too lazy or too scared to do the very demanding work of embracing pain—for contrary to what some believe, dealing with emotions is *very* hard work!—or it could be that we are afraid of other hurts we might lay bare if we honestly confront the sources of our distress. For often, when we are honest with our feelings, we find that accompanying our pain are clusters of other strong feelings that may include differing combinations of anger, guilt, rage, sadness, insecurity, disappointment, loneliness, confusion... the list is long. When we are rigorously honest, we may suddenly find ourselves struggling with many more open questions than we anticipated. We may feel bogged down in analyzing and working through these many-faceted clusters of feelings. *Yet we must embrace these feelings no matter how painful.*

When we realize the extreme demands of embracing pain, we can find the courage to face them by remembering our ultimate goal: determining our best response to our hurts and learning the lessons taught us through our struggles (as we shall see later).

Alone with Pain

It is during the earliest stages of our honest recognition of our pain (in which we may identify other feeling clusters and the sources of our pain) that we may feel the most alone, hurt, misunderstood, and tempted with giving up. It seems that no one really cares or understands. Sometimes even God seems distant!

At stressful times like these it is helpful to know that other persons who have possessed great faith have felt this same way. Several of the Psalms give us insight into what it feels like to be in this lonely and bitter place where we embrace and wrestle with pain. In fact, an entire group of Psalms, called the "laments," reveals the struggles of the psalmists in understanding their own suffering as they too asked, "Where are you, God?" Just a few of their words, ones resonating with our feelings:

> How long, O Lord? Wilt thou
>   forget me for ever?
> How long wilt thou hide thy
>   face from me?
> How long must I bear pain in my soul,
>   and have sorrow in my heart all the day?
>   Psalm 13:1−2

My wounds grow foul and fester
    because of my foolishness,
I am utterly bowed down and prostrate;
    all the day I go about mourning.

I am utterly spent and crushed;
    I groan because of the tumult of my heart.

Psalm 38:5–6, 8

I say to God, my rock:
    "Why hast thou forgotten me?
Why go I mourning
    because of the oppression of the enemy?"
As with a deadly wound in my body,
    my adversaries taunt me,
While they say to me continually,
    "Where is your God?"

Psalm 42:9–10

Although there are many times when the words of the Bible offer us inspiration and comfort, at other times they will not immediately soothe our feelings of loneliness in suffering.

In our own time, this reality has been expressed by William Sloane Coffin, pastor of Riverside Church in New York, when he lost his twenty-four-year-old son, Alex, in a tragic automobile accident. In an amazing gesture of courage and openness, not even two weeks after Alex's death, Coffin preached a sermon in which he shared part of his own grieving process with his congregation. Among the flood of sympathy letters he received were many from fellow ministers who, Coffin said, often "proved they knew their Bibles better than the human condition." He found little comfort, he said, from those who sought to give help by proclaiming that it was "God's will" for Alex to die. Coffin continued:

> The point is this: while the words of the Bible are
> true, grief renders them unreal. The reality of grief
> is the absence of God—"My God, my God, why hast

thou forsaken me?" The reality of grief is the solitude of pain, the feeling that your heart's in pieces, your mind's a blank, that "there is no joy the world can give like that it takes away" (Lord Byron).

The most painful reality of our struggles is the knowledge that no one else (including God) can suffer our pain for us. We feel alone in our pain.

Pain and the Cross

No matter who you are or no matter how much faith you may have (or not have), when you face and embrace your pain you will sometimes echo the psalmists and the Reverend William Sloane Coffin: "Where are you, God?" When we find God and our faith meaningful in our lives, it is perfectly natural, even wonderful that we ask such a question of God— no matter how agonizing it feels to utter the question! It is rather commonly thought that questioning is contrary to faith. Yet honest questioning may well be one of the most positive expressions of deep faithfulness. Doubt and searching questions can only exist where there is a deep level of love and respect—and God loves us and respects us enough to allow our doubts and questions!

The greatest comfort available to us all in our seemingly lonely, desertlike places of pain is remembering that Jesus himself felt the excruciating pain of the cross. (In fact, the word "excruciating" comes from the Latin for "to crucify.") For in his own moment of agony, Jesus, too, cried out the words from Psalm 22, "My God, my God, why hast thou forsaken me?" (Matt. 27:46).

From the cross of Christ and these words he spoke there, we can learn much about God's presence amid the suffering of the world and in our own suffering. For nothing shows us more clearly that suffering and pain are a part of life to be embraced than the way Jesus faced the sorrow he knew was inevitable if he stayed on the path to Jerusalem. He too was tempted with avoiding or escaping the struggle ("Father, if it be possible, let this cup pass from me." [Matt. 26:39]). Who among us has been more painfully honest with God about our feelings? And certainly Jesus did not *want* to suffer the pain he was to embrace. But he went on to say, "not as I will, but as thou wilt." Of course, Jesus suffered an agonizing, humiliating death—seemingly, the most useless pain anyone can suffer!

Yet not only do we learn from the crucifixion that Jesus was tempted with avoiding pain and questioning God's presence; the cross points us toward another very important realization when we consider the question, "Where is God when we suffer?" For through the witness of the life and death of Christ, God sent us a message that God did not spare even Jesus the pain of life and death. Nor, since God *was* Christ, did God spare himself agony. Even when his enormous suffering on a lonely cross overcame Jesus and he gave way to doubt—"My God, my God, why hast thou forsaken me?"— we see by this very act that God was there in the suffering, showing us what God is like. *God shows us in the cross that God is also one who suffers—one who is willing to suffer with us as well as for us!* This does not take away *our* suffering; it shows us that even in our darkest despair, God is there with us. Although God will not take away our suffering, God helps us work through the pain by giving us strength, comfort, hope, and courage. Bishop Mack Stokes said it well:

> Calvary was not new to God. It expressed the heart of God. As soon as there were men [and women] that sinned, hearts that broke, souls that despaired, God's great heart knew the cross that was from the beginning himself. This has been beautifully expressed in the book of Revelation where we read of the Lamb slain from the foundation of the world (Rev. 13:8). So the crucifixion is ever present in the heart of God. And the crucifixion is daily reenacted whenever sin

and sadness flourish. And this too fills us with Godly sorrow and pulls us mightily into the marvelous fellowship with God.

(*Major United Methodist Beliefs*, p. 67)

The popular mystic Kahlil Gibran captured the connection between the no pain, no gain principle and the idea of God as a fellow sufferer in his words on "Pain" in *The Prophet*:

> And a woman spoke, saying, Tell us of Pain.
> And he said:
> Your pain is the breaking of the shell that encloses
> your understanding.
> Even as the stone of the fruit must break, that its
> heart may stand in the sun, so must you know
> pain.
>
> And could you keep your heart in wonder at the
> daily miracles of your life, your pain would
> not seem less wondrous than your joy;
> And you would accept the seasons of your heart,
> even as you have always accepted the seasons
> that pass over your fields.
> And you would watch with serenity through the
> winters of your grief.
>
> Much of your pain is self-chosen.
> It is the bitter potion by which the physician
> within you heals your sick self.
> Therefore trust the physician, and drink his remedy
> in silence and tranquility:
> For his hand, though heavy and hard, is guided by
> the tender hand of the Unseen,
> And the cup he brings, though it burn your lips,
> has been fashioned of the clay which the Potter
> has moistened with His own sacred tears.

"A Curious Paradox"

*W*hen we realize that God has shown us in Christ that God suffers along with us, our pleas to God that we be spared from struggle and pain are understandable in their honesty; yet to expect God to shelter us from suffering is to miss the meaning of suffering taught us by the cross.

One of the paradoxes of life is that we sometimes must hurt before we can grow. Looking a little more closely, we learn that by this same paradox we see the meaning of life through death, joy through sorrow, hope through despair, and love through hate. It is through pain that we see growth, through the cross that we see God.

At the beginning of this book are printed the poignant words spoken at the close of the musical *The Fantasticks*:

> There is a curious paradox
> That no one can explain.
> Who understands the secret
> Of the reaping of the grain?
>
> Who understands why Spring is born
> Out of Winter's laboring pain?
> Or why we all must die a bit
> Before we grow again.

There is a sense in which we will never understand or fully explain why our lives must in part be painful. No matter how earnest our prayers, no matter how penetrating or intelligent our questioning, we will not ever thoroughly know *why*.

But we do know that in the spring the delicate shoots of beautifully budding flowers break the soil left hard and barren from the winter's bitter cold. We know that one tiny planted seed, if nurtured to maturity, yields much more grain than the one originally sacrificed to the ground. We know that a pruned fruit tree will bear more and larger fruit than one left unattended. And we know that our scrapes and cuts and bruises, as well as most of our minor and major surgeries, eventually are made well through the miraculous process we call healing.

The point: That there is manifest in our world a process of hurt and healing, practice and proficiency, pain and gain suggests that this is the process by which God works spiritual growth in our lives. Although God may be responsible, ultimately, in allowing this painful process to enter creation, God remains present throughout this painful process, faithfully nurturing and comforting and giving growth to all of us who live, hurt, struggle, and learn. In our lives, as in the world about us, there must be rain and sunshine, night and day, winter and spring!

Further, to deny pain is to fail to listen to very important communication from God. For pain is the sign given to us telling us we are in danger and must make a response to work our way through the danger by seeking help. When in pain, we know something is wrong that needs to change! Pain is part of—even essential to—the miracle of healing. For our discomfort is an excellent motivation for us to seek help from God, our church, our families and friends, medical and psychological professionals, books, or whatever else may be able to assist us in working through our hurt.

While we struggle, however, pain is not all we feel. God has tossed out a lifeline for us to hold on to: *hope*, which can sustain us and help us pull ourselves toward the shores of progress. And with hope, we also have faith; faith not that we will be spared pain but that God will lead us *through* the pain and struggle to our goal of growth. Therefore, in our struggle to understand God's will, let us not concentrate solely on our pain (although we know we are to accept it). Let us look with hope and faith toward attaining new, richer experience of the precious life God has given us.

Part II: GAIN

For everything there is a season, and a time for every
matter under heaven:
>*a time to be born, and a time to die;*
>. . . . .
>*a time to break down, and a time to build up;*
>*a time to weep, and a time to laugh;*
>*a time to mourn, and a time to dance;*
>. . . . .
>*a time to embrace, and a time to refrain from*
> *embracing.*
>. . . . . . .
What gain has the worker from his toil?
> *(Ecclesiastes 3:1,2a,3b,4,5b,9)*

Discipline and Learning

We have seen that asking God, "Why am I suffering?" is a healthy response to pain, one appropriate to a person who considers God very important; but that seeking God's deliverance from struggle may not be fruitful. Allowing unrelenting questioning to plague one's heart diverts attention and energy from where they need to be placed: on becoming whole.

In embracing our pain we must guard against allowing it to get the best of us—which may happen if we concentrate on what seems to us to be the futility of our struggle. It is crucial for us to realize that when we do this we are allowing our pain to control us: As Leo Buscaglia has written, "When we cling to pain we end up punishing ourselves." Rather, we should learn to manage our pain so that we may move ourselves out of the danger of which our pain warns us.

So instead of intensifying the hurt by calling undue amounts of attention to it, we must work toward focusing our attention on our response to pain—and begin to realize the growth that will result from our efforts.

Having summarized the faith of great persons from the

Old Testament, the writer of Hebrews, using athletic imagery, admonishes us to concentrate on a faithful response to suffering rather than "cling" to it:

> Therefore, since we are surrounded by so great a cloud of witnesses, let us lay aside every weight, and sin which clings so closely, and let us run with perseverance the race that is set before us, looking to Jesus the pioneer and perfecter of our faith, who for the joy that was set before him endured the cross, despising the shame, and is seated at the right hand of the throne of God.
>
> Consider him who endured from sinners such hostility against himself, so that you may not grow weary or fainthearted. In your struggle against sin you have not resisted to the point of shedding your blood. And have you forgotten the exhortation which addresses you as sons?—
> "My son, do not regard lightly the
>   discipline of the Lord,
>   nor lose courage when you are punished
>   by him.
>   For the Lord disciplines him who he loves,
>   and chastises every son whom he
>   receives."
>
> It is for discipline that you have to endure. God is treating you as sons; for what son is there whom a father does not discipline? If you are left without discipline, in which all have participated, then you are illegitimate children and not sons. Besides this, we have had earthly fathers to discipline us and we respected them. Shall we not much more be subject to the Father of spirits and live? For they disciplined us for a short time at their pleasure, but he disciplines us for our own good, that we may share his holiness.

And then the most important part:

> For the moment all discipline seems painful rather

than pleasant; later it yields the peaceful fruit of righteousness to those who have been trained by it.

(Heb. 12:1–11)

The image of the heavenly parent used in this passage may evoke a recollection of the earthly parent who dragged us by the ear out behind the woodshed to warm our seat! Who has not heard a loving parent utter, at just such a "bottom-warming" occasion, "This is going to hurt me more than it hurts you!" Few of those on the literal receiving end believe this parental cliché. Yet strangely, when we become parents who must at times punish our own children, these words about discipline suddenly speak truth.

The original Greek word translated as "discipline" in the scripture passage offered above is derived from the same root word as "to instruct" and "to learn." Therefore, the "discipline" of that passage is not necessarily to be associated exclusively with punishment (although certainly the element of punishment is also present in the passage). Actually, this periscope emphasizes discipline as a learning, growing, deepening experience. In other words, this passage tells us that when we are in the midst of suffering, we should view the "discipline" we find there as an opportunity for spiritual growth rather than as punishment from an angry, capricious parent figure. Although this discipline is painful, later we find that our suffering yields the peaceful righteousness that comes from God.

In his fine book *Where Is God When It Hurts?* Philip Yancey points out that the New Testament describes at least five ways in which suffering can yield spiritual growth. In essence, Yancey says that the role of suffering in our faith is that it "turns us to God" when we might otherwise not have been willing to seek and receive God's help. For suffering, the Bible says, can:

1. Refine our faith   (1 Pet. 1:5–7)
2. Produce maturity of faith   (James 1:2–4)
3. Allow us an opportunity to display God's works
(John 9:10–13)

4. Conform us more nearly to Christ's image
(Rom. 8:28,29)
5. Produce in us Christian perseverance and character
(Rom. 5:3–8)

Let us take a closer look into these areas of spiritual growth.

Refining Faith

*I*n common with the book of Revelation, 1 Peter is a letter written when persecution of the early Christians by the Roman State was rampant. Citizenship in the Roman Empire demanded full allegiance, and Christian loyalty, it was thought, undermined imperial rule. Christians who refused to bow to the royal throne and worship the Caesars as gods (as was often practiced) were severely persecuted, meaning death for many disciples.

Addressing those Christians who were undergoing persecution, the writer of 1 Peter began his letter:

> Blessed be the God and Father of our Lord Jesus Christ! By his great mercy we have been born anew to a living hope through the Resurrection of Jesus Christ from the dead, and to an inheritance which is imperishable, undefiled, and unfading, kept in heaven for you, who by God's power are guarded through faith for a salvation ready to be revealed in the last time.
>
> In this rejoice, though now for a little while you may have to suffer various trials, so that the genuineness of your faith, more precious than gold which though perishable is tested by fire, may rebound to praise and glory and honor at the revelation of Jesus Christ.
>
> (1 Pet. 1:3–7)

Because we are imperfect humans in need of "refinement," like a precious metal requiring purification, we need to be purged of impurities in our faith. The writer compares this purification to the "testing" of gold, which is accomplished only by the "refiner's fire."

We can observe from this passage, however, that the opening admonition of 1 Peter was actually intended as an encouraging reminder to the persecuted to look not at the immediate pain of the fiery testing, but beyond it to the positive results the "various trials" produce:

> Having purified your souls by your obedience to the truth for a sincere love of the brethren, love one another earnestly from the heart. You have been born anew, not of perishable seed but of imperishable, through the living and abiding word of God; for
> "all flesh is like grass
> and all its glory like the
> flower of the grass.
> The grass withers, and the flower falls,
> But the word of the Lord abides for ever."
> That word is the good news which was preached to you.   (1 Pet. 1:22–25)

Speaking of suffering as "fire" is reflective of what we feel when we embrace pain. Fire burns and hurts! But fire also purifies and strengthens, forging toughness and durability. Just as melted gold when purified may be molded into artworks of immortal beauty or jewelry that will last and enhance the owner for years, faith that is refined through struggle with suffering is molded after the likeness of God— the one who has come into our world in the likeness of a sufferer.

From the "refiner's fire," impurities in our faith surface in our consciousness. And having recognized those impurities, we can no longer remain the same. For once we have been tempered by the discipline of dealing with painful occurrences, we can no longer be, for instance, as selfish in our relationships with others or as insensitive to their pain, as we were before. Or we may grow spiritually by learning that when it comes right down to it, we really do not trust God or anyone else. Or we may learn patience simply by *having* to practice it in searching for the roots of our struggle. In all these areas (and many more) the imperfections of our faith come to light in order that we may begin to purify ourselves of them.

Mature Faith

> *Count it all joy, my brethren, when you meet various trials, for you know that the testing of your faith produces steadfastness. And let steadfastness have its full effect that you may be perfect and complete, lacking in nothing.* (Jam. 1:2–4)

For centuries, suffering has been likened to groping in darkness, shivering out in the cold, or being stranded in a desert. Drawing from these rich resources, Martin Marty, in his wonderful book *A Cry of Absence: Reflections for the Winter of the Heart*, corresponds the changing seasons of the year to the seasons of one's spiritual life. When someone close to us dies or we experience some other kind of loss, our spirituality may have a cold wintery feeling (as opposed to a warm summery feeling when things seem to be going well). There are many persons, he says, who claim to be "spirit-filled" who never embrace or even recognize the wintery spirituality because they think it "un-Christian" to let on that things aren't going so well. "Never does the storm of a troubled heart receive its chance to be heard. The Lord satisfied every need, one hears, so it would be a sin to stare once more at the void within. Christ is the answer, the spirit is warm and no chill is ever allowed between the boards or around the windows of the soul."

As Marty suggests, it is too bad that many view denying one's suffering as the most mature and staunchly faithful way to respond to suffering in a Christian manner.

But no: Such a response is an expression of *immature* faith. It presumes that all suffering is evil and that the visitation of pain into our lives is something not to be heeded but only endured! Rather, to fail to cultivate this enormously fruitful ground for spiritual growth is to miss some of the most deeply rewarding experiences in Christian life! Although denial is a necessary coping mechanism imbedded within our souls for dealing with grief, extended denial of pain blocks spiritual and emotional growth. It is immature faith, a faith that meagerly fed and underexercised may eventually peter out altogether.

In James's epistle we read, "Count it all *joy* . . . when you meet various trials." In the previous section we read in 1 Peter, "In this *rejoice*, though now for a little while you may have to suffer various trials." Is the mature response to rejoice while we are in pain?

The words *joy* and *rejoice* as they appear in James and 1 Peter do not mean exactly what one might think at first glance. The rejoicing we find there is not a shallow, Pollyannaish refusal to admit that problems exist; rather, it is the realistic recognition of struggle bolstered by the decision to rejoice in knowing that God is working to bring one safely through the strife.

It is a very difficult achievement to be able to truly rejoice while one is suffering. Most certainly, such rejoicing will not take the form of emotional jubilance or elation. James proclaims that suffering may be counted as joy or gain when one faces the trials because the encounter with pain may produce the quality of *steadfastness*. And steadfastness, when it is allowed to bud and flower into fullness, produces the rarest of all qualities: Christian wholeness and maturity.

True Christian maturity, then, is a steadfastness that we attain not simply by enduring suffering and especially not by denying pain. It is a quality that, like any other maturity, accrues with experience, age, and a lot of willing work. It is the ability to redirect one's thoughts beyond one's own immediate woes to realize the spiritual growth that results from the tests of faith.

Therefore when suffering comes, one "rejoices." Not that one enjoys the pain; but with suffering comes a more mature faith that knows many meaningful insights and new joys await us.

Finding Meaning in Our Trials

> *As he passed by, he saw a man blind from his birth. And his disciples asked him, "Rabbi, who sinned, this man or his parents, that he was born blind?" Jesus answered, "It was not that this man sinned, or his parents, but that the works of God might be made manifest in him.*
> (John 9:1–3)

It was very common in biblical times as in ours, to attempt to blame physical infirmities, diseases, and personal trials on one's own sins or on the "sins of the fathers"—one's parents (see Ezekiel 18:20 and Exodus 20:5, for example). Although it is clear through modern medical diagnosis that indeed some difficulties are hereditary (such as hemophilia and cystic fibrosis) and that certain psychological disorders stem from parental "guidance" (or the lack of it), in the story retold above, Jesus makes it perfectly clear that the blind man's handicap was *not* a punishment for some long forgotten misdemeanor committed by his mother or father.

We saw earlier, in examining a passage from Hebrews, that at times we may think of our difficulties as God's way of disciplining us—teaching us as a parent teaches a child. But Jesus' words to his disciples concerning the blind man give us a clearer understanding of one kind of gain resulting from discipline: that the work of God may be displayed through growth unbounded by our inherent weakness.

Of course, in this story Jesus healed the man of his blindness, and presumably it was the healing of his blindness that manifested the work of God. Many of us who hurt desperately pray to God asking for similarly miraculous healing. Many "Christians" have made a comfortable living peddling such healing. Although much controversy surrounds the issue, many people believe they have indeed been miraculously healed of physical and mental ills. Many other *equally faithful persons* also diligently pray and still do not find themselves healed of their diseases. Do some persons happen to know a magic formula that "works" with God, while others continue to suffer only because of their ignorance? Although no one fully understands the mystery of healing, the God millions of Christians worship and serve is not a God who heals capriciously "on demand." Rather, our thinking about Divine healing needs broadening to include many differing ways in which we may receive healing and wholeness.

The *meaning* we derive from working through suffering rather than the eradication of disease from our bodies ought to be the major criterion by which we perceive "healing." Though one party in a troubled relationship might be terminally ill, the *relationship* might well be healed. Or through dealing with the hurt of infertility, a couple may find healing in accepting that infertility in no way lessens their capacity to love an adopted child. Other healing victories may result from dealing with suffering—many more ways than we have the capacity to imagine or the perception to observe.

I once conducted the funeral of a dear old friend named Grace. Only a few years before, she had experienced the loss of her husband of over fifty years. Only weeks after his burial, she learned that a malignancy was raging through her body. Through magnificent perseverance, while grieving over the loss of her husband, Grace underwent agonizing chemotherapy treatments hoping they would arrest the disease. The treatments failed to halt the spread of the disease.

Yet Grace never gave up hope that one day she would be rid of her cancer.

Her health continued to deteriorate badly, and following her long and valiant struggle, Grace died. As the one who would deliver her eulogy, I agonized over what to say about Grace's death. And I confess I was tempted by questions of why such a marvelous woman had died such a lingering and painful death. Why wasn't *she* healed? If faith and hope were the keys to unlock the door to healing, she certainly possessed them in quantity! But then I began to recall her last few months and all the many persons who came in contact with Grace: There were the many friends who stopped by or telephoned to say hello and encourage her; there was the high school youth group from our church who came Christmas caroling at her home; and there was her family, who surrounded her with their love during those last days. To all of these, Grace's words and actions were always kind and graceful. Even though she did not attempt to hide her intense pain, she also did not hide her hope that healing would come—a hope that never died, even though she did.

At the funeral, it was said of Grace, "This horrible disease may have conquered her body, but *nothing* defeated her spirit, her faith, and her hope!"

As we relate Grace's struggle to be healed with the criterion of *meaning* found in suffering (rather than in physical healing), I cannot help but feel that it was the witness of Grace's death, her clinging on to hope, that proved to be the manifestation of God's healing power! Those people who came to visit Grace as she struggled with cancer did not walk away grumbling about why God had not healed her. They left her presence *inspired* and crucially aware that in Grace they had witnessed God's display of the great power of faith and hope. What a glorious vision of the deeply meaningful ways God is with us in suffering!

Her disease was not contagious, but her hope and faith *were*. And many were healed by witnessing new meaning for themselves through her life and death.

God's power is displayed in the meaning we find in suffering and healing!

Everything Works Together

> Now hope that is seen is not hope. For who hopes for
> what he sees? But if we hope for what we do not see, we
> wait for it with patience.
> Likewise the Spirit helps us in our weakness; for we do
> not know how to pray as we ought, but the Spirit
> himself intercedes for us with sighs too deep for
> words. . . .
> We know that in everything God works for good with
> those who love him, who are called according to his
> purpose.   (Rom. 8:24b, 26, 28)

If God does not necessarily punish us for misconduct, as we have learned in the story of Jesus and the blind man, God also does not necessarily reward us with good things in this life when we are good or faithful. In the Christian faith we affirm God's love and care for every person equally, no matter how good or bad we are.

Although some scriptures, especially in the Old Testament, suggest that we are rewarded for our goodness, it has long been part of the Christian theological tradition that God does not dispense rewards for good behavior as we might hand out treats to a well-behaved pet.

We know that because God cares for us like an earthly parent, God also wants the best for us. Because we know that it rains "on the just and on the unjust," while we also affirm that God naturally wants the best for us, we have a difficult time understanding how God's will operates. And when we are struggling or suffering, we may feel God's will is nowhere in evidence. Yet we read in Romans, "all things work together for good to them that love God."

Probably the best-known book concerning human understanding of God's will is Leslie Weatherhead's classic *The Will of God*. In that series of sermons, originally prepared for members of his congregation in London who were suffering the tragic consequences of World War II, Weatherhead suggested we use the words "the will of God" too loosely. We confuse ourselves by not understanding the many differing ways in which God's will is expressed and how that will works in our lives. Too often we think of God's will as being a narrow path down which we must dutifully trod. And if we choose a wrong fork in the road, we are consigned, perhaps irreparably, to the hazards of a life other than the one that God *intended* for us. Our wrong choice, we believe, is the source of all our distress.

To clarify these differing misunderstandings about God's will, Weatherhead suggested thinking of God's will in three aspects: God's *intentional* will, God's *circumstantial* will, and God's *ultimate* will.

Confusion prevails when we attribute *one aspect* of God's will to all our lives. We generally think God's will is naturally God's *intention*. But we also believe God loves us. So how can God both love us yet *intend* bad things to happen to us, especially when we try to to be good people? This confusion is apparent when a widow, for instance, speaks of her husband's death as his having been "taken" (implying, according to her perception, that God did the "taking"). Or we see confusion in another man (a faithful member of a church) who when his musically talented daughter committed suicide gained some kind of contorted comfort in telling persons attending the funeral that "God must have needed another soprano in his heavenly choir."

In Matthew 18:14 Jesus said, "It is not the will of my Father who is in heaven that one of these little ones should perish." From this scripture and many others, one may assume that it is not God's *intention* for little ones (nor, presumably, any of the rest of us) to suffer or perish. Yet we know all too well that we do. Why?

Because humans are free to serve and follow God, we are

also free to choose what is sinful or evil. And some of the sinful choices we make cause suffering for ourselves and others. Yet even within these evil or sinful *circumstances* brought about through our exercising the freedom God lovingly grants us as human beings, God still wills us to choose what is worthy (putting us on the better track toward godliness) rather than choose that which would cause further evil and suffering. So even in the worst of circumstances, when we have made the worst choices, God has a *circumstantial* will for us—one that may be a bit different from God's original intention.

Even though God allows the original *intentional* will to be thwarted (in order that we may freely choose to love and follow God) through circumstances brought about by our freedom, we above all believe that God's *ultimate* will cannot be thwarted. Of course, God's ultimate will for creation is not yet fully realized (although we believe it is realized in part). But in faith we know and hope that God's ultimate will can come to pass on earth as well as heaven. Indeed, this is our prayer when we repeat the Lord's Prayer, "Thy will be done on earth as it is in heaven."

Such an orientation helps us understand that sometimes we suffer because God loves us enough to give us the freedom to make mistakes. Without this freedom, we would be mere puppets with God pulling the strings. God loves but does not manipulate. Truly, God's perfect knowledge must "hurt God more than it hurts us." For the Almighty is certainly powerful enough to halt suffering—but because God loves us enough to give us freedom, God chooses to allow us to hurt and grow. And this is the way God has been shown to us in Christ.

The most vivid example of this principle and of Weatherhead's differentiation between God's intentional will, circumstantial will, and ultimate will may be seen in the life, death, and Resurrection of Christ. However, in Christ's life we may see that it *was not* God's initial intention that Christ come to die (we sometimes hear the prayer "Thank you, God, for sending Christ to die"), else why did Jesus travel, teach, and gather a discipleship, exhorting his hearers, "Follow me...." It was God's intention that Jesus' hearers should repent, believe, and become a part of the new "kingdom," not kill him! And this kingdom, should Jesus have been followed according to God's intention, would have set in motion a revolutionary agent in our world by which the principle of love would have banished hatred, justice would have displaced inequality, and mercy would have overcome vengeance. Because of the freedom granted by God and the subsequent evil choices made by humans insensitive to God's intention— as God knew they might be—the *circumstances* arose in which Jesus was required to make a very important decision: He could either quit proclaiming the truth about God's love and human sinfulness or bear the consequences of human sinfulness by allowing himself to be killed on the cross. Although it was not God's *initial* intention that humankind reject and crucify the Messiah, the world was free to do so—and so inclined. Thus it became God's *circumstantial* will for Christ to die, in order to show the world both the depth of human sinfulness and the breadth of God's love.

The cross—the seemingly final sign of defeat for God's will in the world—became in itself an expression of God's ultimate will being accomplished. For God's *ultimate* will, a reconciliation between God and humanity, was accomplished in the outcome of the crucifixion: *Resurrection.* For in the Resurrection we see most fully God expressing the reality of hope within our world. When all seemed like death and suffering on the cross, life and hope and faith and joy exploded in the triumph of Resurrection. It is the hope of the Resurrection that allows us to endure and seek wholeness while we suffer, for now we know the crosses we bear will see us resurrected into joy and victory.

This understanding of God's will helps us realize a very important spiritual gain amid our strife. For with the apostle Paul, when we affirm that "all things work together for good," we are not saying that no circumstances arise that are not difficult or emotionally and spiritually trying. *Faith is no insurance policy against tragedy!* Yet the words of Paul come to us in our struggle, representing hope that God's ultimate will will not be denied. Through faith in God and the understanding that the divine gift of reason provides, we may have confidence that here, even in the dark night of the soul, in circumstances that seem far from the love and care God may intend, *God will help work things out*. We may not understand how. We do not need to. But with the help of hope, we may enjoy the privilege of witnessing God's wonderful power working in ways we could not possibly have anticipated.

Beginnings of Hope

> *Therefore, since we are justified by faith, we have peace with God through our Lord Jesus Christ. Through him we have obtained access to this grace in which we stand, and we rejoice in our hope of sharing the glory of God. More than that, we rejoice in our sufferings, knowing that suffering produces endurance, and endurance produces character, and character produces hope, and hope does not disappoint us, because God's love has been poured into our hearts through the Holy Spirit which has been given to us.* (Rom. 5:1–5)

Our spiritual passage from suffering through endurance to character leading to hope that "does not disappoint us" is a long perilous journey. Yet one of the greatest gains we can find in our struggle is to anchor ourselves in the reality of God's love for us. Then we have all the strength and hope we need to face whatever trials we encounter.

At the beginning of the path to hope, however, lies suffering. And it is only in the midst of suffering that we truly find endurance and character and the beginnings of hope.

The lives of countless persons stand as witness to the fact that struggle with suffering is redemptive. Although most persons engage in the struggle unwillingly, they learn through painful experience the truths taught by biblical passages we have examined.

One person whose eventual growth came about through

much suffering was a young man named Jim. Although he was bright and talented, because he always had his own way and things had generally gone well for him, he was frankly rather spoiled. His parents, like most, had wanted the best for their child; they lavished upon Jim just about everything he wanted, to the point where he expected nearly everything to be given to him.

As it came time for him to graduate from high school and decide upon college and a vocation, he decided that college was too much work and got a job working for a contracting firm. His abrupt decision bitterly disappointed his parents, who had long planned and budgeted so that he could attend a university. Some people wondered aloud whether Jim *intended* to hurt his parents.

Though Jim had made his decision, he lacked a basic direction for his life. He met a young woman and they soon became engaged to be married. But Jim became growingly disillusioned and bitter that his life as an adult seemed to consist of financial problems, work that he had found meaningless, and a future holding few prospects for improvement.

Life came crashing down on him the day he fell off an iron beam suspended more than fifty feet above the ground. Suddenly Jim found himself in a hospital with an injured spine leaving him a paraplegic. If he had been somewhat bitter before the accident, you can imagine the anger, frustration, and hopelessness he felt as he was forced into making an adjustment to such a profoundly difficult handicap.

Yet Jim was equipped with the tools he needed to fight the handicap; for despite his "attempt at hurting them," he had a supportive family, many friends who expressed their caring, and most important, he came to find he had a deep desire to struggle with his pain and realize gain.

It was not ever easy. Jim spent nearly six months in the hospital engaged in therapy that produced much pain and agonizingly slow progress. During those days of therapy, Jim had no choice but to remain in his bed, dependent on those around him. He was forced to accept that there were many things he could not do for himself. His physical powerlessness necessitated that a constant vigil be kept at his bedside. His parents and fiancée, taking turns in this service, were with him constantly, and Jim was forced to converse with them and with others who cared for him. Many friends brought cards and gifts and words of encouragement. Persons from his church also came by to offer their support and help.

Even though these many persons came by to help, Jim struggled continually with feelings of anger, bitterness, and resentment about his accident. He tried to keep his emotions bottled up inside, but there were many times he couldn't. At times he cried and rammed his fist into the pillow. He was often cross with the nurses and others who tried to help him. One day, exasperated by the constancy of the work it required to learn to cope with his paralysis, at the very edge of his endurance, Jim lashed out at a visitor from his church. Seething with resentment, he shouted, "Don't even try to talk about God to me! I don't care. Where was God when I fell? Where's God *now*!?"

The friend wasn't sure what to say, but managed to reply, "I wish I knew why you have to go through this, but I don't. But please know that God is with you and that when you fell, God was right there hurting with you! And God's with you now, helping you to get stronger."

Unlike such scenes in the movies, no fireworks went off and no climactic music accented the experience. Jim was still angry; yet this conversation was a turning point for him. He kept on working at his therapy and gradually improved. Jim never regained the use of his legs, but he learned to function proficiently in his wheelchair.

But the most strikingly miraculous part of Jim's healing process, indeed his most successful therapy, was the change in his attitude toward life. Before the accident and during therapy, Jim showed the world a sour personality that tended to repel others. But caring people stayed with him and helped him despite his bitterness. Slowly, through the process of fighting his disability, Jim began to realize that nothing in life could be taken for granted. He grew to appreciate those who cared for him rather than assume someone always would be there to provide for his needs. Even though he came to recognize the painful reality that he could never again use his legs, he also realized that he could *decide* what his attitude toward his circumstances would be. Little things suddenly meant a great deal to him. The cards, visits, and words of encouragement that Jim had scorned at first became important to him as he learned to appreciate these gestures of care and love. Jim also realized God is not far off but nearby, giving courage, comfort, and support.

Jim's story is full of pain and gain. It remains (and always will remain) painful for him that he will never again enjoy the full use of his legs. But another healing came to Jim, a deeper fulfillment in life, one he may never have known had he not experienced his tragic accident.

Jim found through his painful recovery a new assurance in himself. Not long after Jim and Jenny were married, he began his own small firm and has found his venture successful and rewarding. Although now, years later, life continues to be a struggle, Jim lives it to the fullest.

The kinds of gains to be found through dealing with pain are as many as the persons who truly embrace their pain. We must all, individually, seek out and identify those possibilities for spiritual growth toward which our pain points us. To be sure, someone is trying to teach us lessons. But it is up to us to learn!

Yet while we learn, what motivates us to continue in the always arduous, sometimes long struggle? Where can we find the strength we need to continue?

Through *hope*.

Part III: HOPE

When we become aware that we do not have to escape
our pains, but that we can mobilize them into a common
search for life, those very pains are transformed from
expressions of despair into signs of hope.

—Henri Nouwen

Hope and the Human Spirit

There is a crack of time, wedged between our experience of discipline and pain and the time when we feel something of the benefits of spiritual gain, when we may find it especially difficult to persist during our struggles. During this time, when we still have not attained our goals despite our having invested great amounts of energy in trying to resolve our problems, we again find ourselves confronted with difficult choices between faith and doubt, growth and decline, hope and despair. We feel we have come too far to give up, yet, are too weary from the struggle to continue.

During this troublesome phase, the cultivation of a hopeful attitude is crucial. For now, as we engage in our struggles, our temptation becomes strong to allow our attitudes to fluctuate between hope and despair. Each of us possesses a personal tolerance level for pain, and the circumstances surrounding our struggles vary. Do your own experience, background, and general outlook on life encourage a hopefulness toward the outcome of your trials? Or do you tend to approach struggle with an inward conviction that fate cannot be altered? Surrendering one's attitude toward "fate," or to a misunderstanding of God's will, may well deepen one's sense of having become a hopeless victim of circumstances perceived to be raging beyond control.

Our attitude toward hope, healing, and wholeness will greatly influence the speed and scope of the spiritual growth we derive from the discipline of dealing with pain. And the key ingredient in our approach to distress during this significant time is the mental and spiritual discipline of hope.

Many groups of people throughout history have learned the value of hope while enduring difficult, seemingly impossible times. From his study of such peoples, in particular those whose sufferings are recounted in the Old Testament, Walter Brueggemann has concluded, "Hope comes out of the public processing of pain."

From the terrifyingly gruesome and dehumanizing persecution of the European Jewish community during the insanely anti-Semitic reign of the Nazis have come many startling realizations about the human potential for evil. Yet from the valiant struggle of this people against evil; from the inexpressibly profound pain that has been processed in the years since the Holocaust—and continues to be processed by Jews and non-Jews—many positive contributions have been made to our understanding of the resiliency of the human spirit and the importance of hope.

Among the many moving personal accounts written by survivors of the Nazi death camps is Viktor Frankl's *Man's Search for Meaning*. While Frankl recounts his experiences at the personal level, he is also remarkably able, from his viewpoint as a trained, professional psychiatrist, to analyze and interpret his own feelings. He vividly details the constant threat of extinction that permeated the lives of death camp residents. They found themselves suddenly stripped of personal possessions and individual identity; and the stench from flesh-burning furnaces ever reminded them that death was as close as any minor infraction of the camp rules—or closer, according to the whims of one's captors. The Nazi death machine very efficiently pushed the experience of human suffering past any fathomable expectation of mental tolerance or physical survival.

How did some survive?

Frankl suggests that the secret not only of the prisoners' survival but also of their spiritual growth was the attitude of hope for the future.

Borrowing from the thought of Nietzsche— "He who has a *why* to live can bear with almost any *how*"—Frankl developed the understanding that even in the worst circumstances imaginable, indeed when one literally has nothing left, *no one, or nothing that happens to you, can control your own spiritual posture concerning your response to the circumstances in which you find yourself!* Frankl wrote:

> We who lived in concentration camps can remember the men who walked through the huts comforting others, giving away their last piece of bread. They may have been few in number, but they offer sufficient proof that everything can be taken from a man but one thing: to choose one's attitude in any given set of circumstances, to choose one's own way.
>
> Naturally, only a few people were capable of reaching great spiritual heights. But a few were given the chance to attain human greatness even through their apparent worldly failure and death, an accomplishment which in ordinary circumstances they would never have achieved. To the others of us, the mediocre and the half-hearted, the words of Bismarck could be applied: "Life is like being at the dentist. You always think that the worst is still to come, and yet it is already over." Varying this, we could say that most men in a concentration camp believed the real opportunities of life had passed. Yet, in reality, there was an opportunity and a challenge. One could make a victory of those experiences, turning life into an inner triumph, or one could ignore the challenge and simply vegetate.

We learn from Frankl that many of those who survived

(and many of those who did not) distinguished themselves in their suffering by accepting hopefully the challenges to growth and human dignity set before them in a world turned upside down. What made the difference was their hope—and their courage.

We cannot, must not hope to find any manner of *justification* for such suffering in terms of "valuable lessons" learned from it. Yet learn from it we must—learn, among other indelible lessons, that God has breathed into the human spirit *the ability to hope—even in the worst of circumstances.* And through hope, the human spirit is motivated to struggle mightily against agents of pain and suffering.

As we have seen, pain is a signal warning that we are in some kind of physical, emotional, or spiritual danger; struggle, with its painful discipline, is the way by which we move through the trials to healing, meaning, and wholeness. And in this crucial crack of time between embracing our pain and attaining wholeness, we can *choose* whether or not we will adopt the attitude of hope.

As persons such as Dr. Frankl show us, hope is not automatically granted to all those who struggle. But it is *available* to all those who are *willing*, through discipline, to process their pain.

Grief and Hope

*F*or several years a large number of persons in the helping professions have contributed much to our understanding of the grief process when we experience a significant loss. Most researchers and writers describe certain stages we predictably pass through in grieving. Because we have spent great amounts of time and emotional energy in nurturing relationships that are of immense value to the enrichment of our lives, when we suffer a loss we must adjust ourselves to the loss of this relationship or value by working through these stages of grief and adjustment; otherwise we may never return to "normal."

Although we do not necessarily advance through these stages in a neatly prescribed order, we can speak of a general progression of the feelings a person typically experiences while grieving. At first we feel shocked and may want to deny or avoid our feelings. We then experience the expression of our emotions, which may also manifest themselves in physical ailments or a sense of panic. We probably feel anger or guilt or a host of other emotions. Finally, usually toward the latter stages of our grief, we begin to feel hope gradually breaking through.

As we can see, hope is not the only feeling we have as we struggle toward acceptance of our loss. Most important, we note that hope does not appear early to illuminate the path we are to take on the journey to wholeness. Hope comes through *gradually*, fading in and out, struggling with all the other feelings we are having; together, those feelings will help us determine our response to the pain, separation, and loneliness we feel.

Although all the emotions we feel as we work through pain are valid, even invaluable, hope is our best friend. For it is hope that motivates us to keep on trying when we feel like quitting; it is hope that the hurt will be relieved that allows us to cry one more time even when we feel that the rivers of tears we have already shed have accomplished little; it is hope that helps us to reach out and openly share our pain with another person even when we feel we want never again to invest our trust in anyone else. It is hope that helps us work to untangle the web of twisted emotions we have tried to bury deep within our being. Hope is a struggle, but it is the struggle to free ourselves from entrapment in this web of complex and unpleasant feelings so that we may be at liberty to live a life of richly satisfying growth.

So to hope *is* to grieve and to grieve *is* to hope!

But where do we find hope?

The Road Less Traveled: God's Hope Displayed

Like all of us who struggle, suffer, learn, and grow, the human characters portrayed in many biblical stories were forced to apprehend the meaning of hope derived from painful situations in their own lives. Such stories (found in both the Old and New Testaments) that illuminate the meaning of hope are too numerous to summarize here; but we can look into several that might help us understand more fully the meaning of hope as we struggle to affirm our reality today.

> That very day two of them were going to a village named Emmaus, about seven miles from Jerusalem, and talking with each other about all these things that had happened. While they were talking and discussing together, Jesus himself drew near and went with them. But their eyes were kept from recognizing him. And he said to them, "What is this conversation which you are holding with each other as you walk?" And they stood still, looking sad. Then one of them, named Cleopas, answered him, "Are you the only visitor to Jerusalem who does not know the things that have happened there in these days?" And he said to them, "What things?" And they said to him, "Concerning Jesus of Nazareth, who was a prophet mighty in deed and word before God and all the people, and how our chief priests and rulers delivered him up to be condemned to death, and crucified him. *But we had hoped that he was the one to redeem Israel.* Yes, and besides all this, it is now the third day since this happened. Moreover, some women of our company amazed us. They were at the tomb early in the morning and did not find his body; and they came back saying that they had even seen a vision of angels, who said that he was alive. Some of those who were with us went to the tomb, and found it just as the women had said; but him they did not see." And he said to

them, "O foolish men, and slow of heart to believe all that the prophets have spoken! Was it not necessary that Christ should suffer these things and enter into his glory?" And beginning with Moses and all the prophets, he interpreted to them in all the scriptures the things concerning himself.

So they drew near to the village to which they were going. He appeared to be going further, but they constrained him, saying, "Stay with us, for it is toward evening and the day is now far spent." So he went in to stay with them. When he was at the table with them, he took the bread and blessed, and broke it, and gave it to them. And their eyes were opened and they recognized him; and he vanished out of their sight. They said to each other, "Did not our hearts burn within us while he talked to us on the road, while he opened to us the scriptures?" And they rose that same hour and returned to Jerusalem; and they found the eleven gathered together and those who were with them, who said, "The Lord has risen indeed, and has appeared to Simon!" Then they told what had happened on the road, and how he was known to them in the breaking of the bread.

(Luke 24:13–35 italics added)

For the disciples, too, there was that crack of time when they were tempted to give up hope. In the mere passing of a week, they had entered Jerusalem with Jesus in triumph, only to have their hopes dashed to despair in witnessing their leader's agonizing, ignominious death upon the cross. They were severely hurt and disillusioned: Jesus, the one in whom they put their hope to deliver their nation, was dead!

The two disciples walking on the road from Jerusalem to Emmaus felt hopeless. They had heard Jesus was raised from the dead, but no one had seen him. So they moped back to Emmaus, grief-stricken, bewildered, and grievously smitten in their loss of hope.

Of course, when they complained to the stranger—Jesus,

whom they failed to recognize—he told them of the *necessity* of Christ's suffering and interpreted to them "all the scriptures concerning himself." Yet it was not until Jesus entered their home and broke bread with them that they finally recognized him *and understood who he truly was and what had happened to him.*

The disciples immediately arose and journeyed a road much less traveled—the *hopeful* road from Emmaus back to Jerusalem. Unlike their travels earlier in the day on that same road coming to Emmaus, *this* trip to Jerusalem was filled with a freshly renewed hope and joy from the disciples' having seen and experienced the most hopeful sign God has ever given to our world—the resurrected Christ!

As we learned in the section "Pain and the Cross," Jesus' death was in part God's message to us that God is with us in our painful difficulties, suffering with us and for us. Similarly, the Resurrection of Jesus completes this story begun with his life and suffering death. For in beholding the entire Christ event—Jesus's life, death, and Resurrection—we see that pain and struggle are not all that we are to experience in our Christian lives. Through the Resurrection we see how God *redeems* and *reclaims* suffering and struggle and painful discipline, bringing them to a hopeful and joyous end! Of course, this does not negate the cross or its redemptive pain. Rather, through the Resurrection, God moves us *through* the pain of the cross to a newer, deeper experience of God's love.

We understand that through this pivotal event in history, God has released a mighty force into our world of struggle. The event represents hope that even in earthly life, we too will be "resurrected" from our pain and struggle, whose rigors have made us "die a bit"—"resurrected" and lifted to greater spiritual heights. The Resurrection gives us faith that even in our darkest hours, the penetrating rays of hope are never far away and will break through to illuminate our life and allow us to "run a little bit farther" down the road.

It seems we journey down the road between Emmaus and Jerusalem many times on our spiritual pilgrimage. We know it as a road of both pain and joy, both disillusionment and certainty, both despair and hope. But the longer we travel this road, the more thoroughly we are convinced that it is the same road viewed from opposite directions. In one direction we feel sorrow and pain; the other direction we may travel is hope.

The story of Christ's Resurrection teaches us that in the midst of our struggle, we have the option of taking the "road less traveled"—the road from Emmaus back to Jerusalem; the journey of hope. And on that road, we find that our pain and despair are redeemed.

The Hope of God's People

There is a sense in which we are always in that crack of time when we travel the Emmaus-Jerusalem road, with its ever-lurking temptation toward hopelessness. Other biblical stories convey this truth to us because we recognize that they are mirrors of our own frustrations and struggles. We have seen in the "lament" Psalms the despairing cry of the psalmist who wonders where God has gone and even questions God's wisdom in allowing such pain and suffering to exist in the world. Yet just as we see the message of pain, gain, and hope revealed in the words of the New Testament writings, we see hope portrayed also in the Psalms and in the history of God's people, the Israelites. Their story, told in the Old Testament, relates not only their questioning of God, it displays also the great trust they felt that in the end God would act to deliver Israel (as well as the individual sufferer) from pain and distress and grant her new life.

This passage from despair to hope often takes place within a particular Psalm. For example in chapter 1 we read from Psalm 13:

> How long, O Lord? Wilt thou
> forget me for ever?

How long wilt thou hide thy
    face from me?
How long must I bear pain in my soul,
    and have sorrow in my heart all the day?
(Ps. 13:1–2)

But the Psalm continues in hope:

But I have trusted in thy steadfast love;
    my heart shall rejoice in thy salvation.
I will sing to the Lord,
    because he has dealt bountifully with me.
(Ps. 13:5–6)

We also looked at the 38 Psalm:

My wounds grow foul and fester
    because of my foolishness,
I am utterly bowed down prostrate;
    all the day I go about mourning.

I am utterly spent and crushed;
    I groan because of the tumult of my heart.
(Ps. 38:5–6, 8)

But the Psalm continues in hope:

But for thee, O Lord, do I wait;
    it is thou, O Lord my God, who wilt answer.

For I am ready to fall,
    and my pain is ever with me.

Do not forsake me, O Lord!
    O my God, be not far from me!
Make haste to help me,
    O Lord, my salvation.
(Ps. 38:15, 17, 21–22)

And Psalm 42:

> I say to God, my rock:
>   "Why hast thou forgotten me?
> Why go I mourning because of the oppression of
>   the enemy?"
> As with a deadly wound in my body,
>   my adversaries taunt me,
> while they say to me continually,
> "Where is your God?"
>
> (Ps. 42:9–10)

But the Psalm continues in hope:

> Why are you cast down, O my soul,
>   and why are you disquieted within me?
> *Hope in God*; for I shall again praise him,
>   my help and my God.
>
> (Ps. 42:11 italics added)

Revealed in these scriptures is a dual recognition of pain and distress, along with a strong expression of resolve to place hope in God.

The roots of hope run deep in ancient Israel's history. And the very basis for the hope of God's people is placed in one pivotal event: the Exodus of the Israelites from Egypt into the Promised Land. A very short time passed between Jesus' Crucifixion and his Resurrection; but the ancient pilgrims wandered in the wilderness longing and hoping for the Promised Land for forty years! Before undertaking this miserably long journey, God's people spent many years as slaves in Egypt, crying out for God to hear them. Many who started the journey never saw its completion.

All generations of Jewish people since then have remembered and celebrated God's deliverance of their ancestors (and thereby themselves as well) from bondage in Egypt. The remembrance of this historical event has provided the primary basis for belief in hope that pervades Jewish thought—and provides invaluable help to Christian thought as well. For not only can Jewish people remember and celebrate the deliverance of their forefathers and foremothers; through this remembrance they also celebrate *their own* present deliverance from bondage, pain, and oppression. Time after time the biblical witness recalls this focal event in history as if it were being relived in the present (see Ps. 80:8, Judg. 6:7–9, 1 Sam. 10:17–18, Josh. 24:16–17). This continual process of dealing with pain and celebrating deliverance has produced a history of hope unequaled in our world.

The basic hope that God would deliver God's people allowed the prophet Jeremiah to proclaim to those persons who were suffering the separation and pain of exile in a foreign land:

> I will fulfill to you my promise and bring you back to this place. For I know the plans I have for you, says the Lord, plans for *shalom* and not for evil, to give you a future and a hope.... You will seek me and find me; when you seek me with all your heart, I will be found by you, says the Lord, and I will restore your fortunes....   (Jer. 29:10–14)
> (Translation from *Living Toward a Vision*, Walter Brueggemann, New York: United Church Press, 1982.)

That vision of peace (*shalom*) includes love, hope, faith, fulfillment, justice, mercy, and many more qualities. But those who suffer find in it what sufferers have found there for many centuries: a vision of hope and meaning in life. We are God's people, and despite evidence to the contrary, God has *not* forgotten us, and will remain faithful.

Yet quite disconcertingly, Jeremiah also notes:

> But seek the *shalom* of the city where I have sent you into exile, and pray to the Lord on its behalf, for in its *shalom* you will find your *shalom*.   (Jer. 29:7)
> (Tr. from *Living Toward a Vision*)

50

This ancient truth startles those of us who wrestle with the spiritual struggles of our own personal "exile" or "bondage." For in Jeremiah, and ultimately in our own life, we learn that it is in the very midst of the exile that we learn the lessons God teaches about wholeness and wellness (*shalom*). In this struggle, which we by no means enjoy, we also, surprisingly, find an unexpected gift: peace, meaning, and spiritual well-being—*shalom*.

We can see that the hope God gave to the people of Israel was the same hope that He displayed in Christ: God is present in the world, actively working through our suffering to offer hope and healing. But as we have seen, it is not hope for deliverance from suffering but hope in deliverance *through* pain and discipline.

Endless Hope?

Jesus' words from Psalm 22, uttered on the cross, "My God, my God, why hast thou forsaken me?" also end in hope affirmed by his Resurrection.

Here is some of the remainder of Psalm 22:

> But thou, O Lord, be not far off!
>> O thou my help, hasten to my aid!
>
> From thee comes my praise in the great
>> congregation,
>> my vows I will pay before those who fear him.
> The afflicted shall eat and be satisfied;
>> those who seek him shall praise the Lord!
> May your hearts live for ever!
>
> All the ends of the earth shall remember and turn
>> to the Lord;

And all the families of the nations shall worship
> before him.
For dominion belongs to the Lord,
> and he rules over the nations.

Yea, to him shall all the proud of the earth bow
> down;
> before him shall bow all who go down to the
> dust,
> and he who cannot keep himself alive.

Posterity shall serve him;
> men shall tell of the Lord
> to the coming generation,
and proclaim his deliverance to a people yet
> unborn,
that he has wrought it.

> (Ps. 22:19, 25–31)

When it may have seemed like Jesus was speaking of a
hopeless end to his life, we see from the Psalm quoted that
he was also proclaiming an endless hope. It is a hope to be
passed from one generation to the next with its one basic
message: God delivers God's people! And through this process
of deliverance, God's people grow in spirit.

Indeed, this hope has been passed to us today through
many generations, and we see it well in the lives of many
persons around us. We earlier saw hope in the life of Jim in
his struggle with his accident as we also saw hope in Grace's
life as she fought a terminal disease.

And you remember William Sloane Coffin's sermon
delivered shortly after the death of his son, Alex.

Coffin concluded his sermon that day,

And of course I know, even when pain is deep,
that God is good. "My God, my God, why hast thou
forsaken me?" Yes, but at least, "My God, my God";
and the psalm only begins that way, it doesn't end

that way. As the grief that once seemed unbearable begins to turn now to bearable sorrow, the truths of the right biblical passages are beginning, once again, to take hold: "Cast thy burden upon the Lord and He shall strengthen thee"; "Weeping may endure for a night, but joy cometh in the morning"; "Lord, by that favor thou has made my mountain to stand strong"; "for thou has delivered my soul from death, mine eyes from tears, and my feet from falling." "In this world ye have tribulation, but be of good cheer, I have overcome the world." "The light shines in darkness, and the darkness has not overcome it."

And finally I know that when Alex beat me to the grave, the finish line was not Boston Harbor in the middle of the night. If a week ago Monday a lamp went out, it was because, for him at least, the Dawn had come.

So I shall—so let us all—seek consolation in that love which never dies, and find peace in the dazzling grace that always is.

Our *hope* as we face the difficulties of life is in the never-ending love God has shown our world.

Part IV: HELP

We do not exist for ourselves (as the center of the universe), and it is only when we are fully convinced of this fact that we begin to love ourselves properly and thus also love others. What do I mean by loving ourselves properly? I mean, first of all, desiring to live, accepting life as a very great gift and a great good, not because of what it gives us, but because of what it enables us to give others.

—*Thomas Merton*

Helpful Prayer

In this process of spiritual growth and learning, a higher stage in our development comes in recognizing the infinite number of ways God offers help in our distress. Among these channels through which we receive God's help, the most direct dimension of assistance comes through prayer.

We acknowledged in the first chapter that we sometimes feel "alone with pain," since no one else can suffer or grow for us. And here's another truth: No matter how alone we may feel, we are never truly alone in our suffering. For when we feel alone and long for help from the Source of all growth and hope, God's presence fulfills our yearning through the discipline of prayer.

However, the kind of help many of us seek through prayer is burdened with misunderstandings. Too often prayer is likened to the presentation of our own personal shopping list to a celestial Santa Claus who promptly delivers the goodies in neatly wrapped packages. And if the packages don't arrive exactly as we asked, and right on our schedule, we nag more diligently until we either get what we wanted or give up! Obviously, this is not true prayer.

Although petitioning God for our needs is certainly part of healthy prayer, true communication with God is infinitely more meaningful and powerful. When we learn and begin to yield to prayer as communication *from* God rather than as a shopping spree, we instantaneously open ourselves to profoundly satisfying and healing experiences of God's help.

To write or read about the elusive experience of God through prayer is an incredibly imprecise task. For in speaking of something so mysterious and personal, words become clumsy almost spurious tools in communicating the meaning of a deep relationship and consciousness of God. Even so it might be helpful to attempt an outline of some general guidelines for prayer.

The long and rich history of literature about the experience of prayer has in recent years exploded with renewed interest. Among the many aspects of prayer that have received much discussion have been the disciplines of silence and solitude, meditation and contemplation, and translating prayer into relationships with others.

In our earlier discussion we stressed discipline, not as a form of punishment but as an opportunity for growth. Just as athletes must "work out" regularly, we must view prayer as the "gymnasium of the soul." But in this arena, most of us feel like weaklings. When it comes to prayer, we assume that we lack the understanding and stamina required to be effective.

The discipline of prayer should not be viewed as a slavish duty to which one must expend every ounce of strength trying to reach an unattainable goal. Rather prayer should be thought of as a liberating discipline that opens doors to greater celebration through receiving God's healing and sustaining presence. Of course, like any other discipline it is difficult (and painful) to grow in prayer. And there is only one way to learn: Pray!

It seems we humans have an inclination to refuse the medicine that can heal us. And because we avoid discipline, we find that, as Douglas Steere wrote, our "greatest pain comes from the tightness of our grip on that which holds us back."

For this reason, while in the midst of our struggle, we

may find it hard to engage the discipline of prayer. In *The Workbook on Intercessory Prayer*, Maxie Dunnam tells of having the same problem. It seems that as he was praying for a retreat he was to lead, excruciating pain throbbed in his shoulders and neck. Because of this discomfort he was not sleeping and having difficulty praying—and release from his pain was part of what he was praying for! Then he said God's word to him was, "until you are relieved of your pain, use it as a call to prayer."

Because our discomfort might be a hindrance to learning the discipline of prayer, I believe this insight of using pain as a "call to prayer" is an excellent one for us to remember. Yet another important element of Dunnam's experience was that his learning did not proceed from what he *told* God but from the word of God to him. It is only in the context of silence and solitude, however, that such insight can come.

To put the problem simply: Most of us are too busy blabbing at God in prayer to ever be able to listen to what God might be "saying" to us. Of course, God doesn't shout audibly in our ears—but most certainly God "speaks" to us, usually in a "whisper." With our verbose prayers, frantic pace of activity, and constant blasting of music in our ears through inventions such as the Walkman, there is little way short of battery failure that we can hear God "whisper."

But making the effort to sustain disciplined silence and solitude with God grants us enormous possibilities for spiritual growth. For in regular aloneness and silence we can more ably discern the "still small voice" whispering in our spiritual ear. Here is where we learn pain's lessons.

This process of communicating and learning in prayer has been called meditation or contemplation. In our first attempts at this type of prayer, (which might be unfamiliar to many of us), we may become discouraged because we find that our minds wander. We start out to pray, but we find ourselves thinking about all sorts of other things—daydreaming! Or we may suddenly realize we are replaying recent conversations or remembering past experiences we either wanted to recall or were trying to forget.

Rather than castigate ourselves for a lack of discipline in retaining "spiritual" thoughts, why not view these images as part of our prayer? From these random thoughts and images may come significant insights and feelings about ourselves and our relationship with God. In this meditation, we may recall and contemplate meaningful scriptures or other readings that have help to offer in our present circumstances. Advice from friends or family members may be placed in our thoughts, giving us encouragement and hope. We may even drift into sleep as a gift of renewal amidst our hard work! The fresh images and energizing insights found in these times are virtually limitless!

In these "depths" of communication with God, you will find that words grow increasingly less important as a tool of communication. Sobs and tears, a grunt of frustration, or a sigh of pain or relief may all be considered nonverbal yet extremely communicative prayer. The apostle Paul expressed this in the following verses:

> Likewise, the Spirit helps us in our weakness; for we do not know how to pray as we ought, but the Spirit himself intercedes for us *with sighs too deep for words.* And he who searches the hearts of men knows what is the mind of the Spirit, because the Spirit intercedes for the saints according to the will of God.
>
> (Rom. 8:26–27 italics added)

Then he reminds us that "we know that in everything God works for good..." (Rom. 8:28).

When "sighs" replace words and communion with God is impressed on us through silence and solitude, meditation and contemplation, one might assume this achievement to equal a constant state of bliss wherein the world's cares are blocked out and can no longer harm us. Paradoxically, this type of prayer leads us not toward strange detachment from the world but a more vital engagement in it. As Henri Nouwen has written, "We are speaking here about a mystery for which words are inadequate. It is the mystery that the heart, which is the center of our being, is transformed by God into his own heart, a heart large enough to embrace the entire universe. Through prayer we can carry in our heart all human pain and sorrow, all conflicts and agonies, all torture and war, all hunger, loneliness, and misery, not because of some great psychological or emotional capacity, but because God's heart has become one with ours."

In reaching inwardly through prayer, we mysteriously find ourselves reaching out to others both to receive their help and to offer help to them.

Helpful People

No one can successfully cope with life's pain and struggle, nor its joys and successes without help from other people and God. Yet many among us apparently believe that living was meant to be a painless activity. Modern-day culture (especially American culture) does its best to brainwash us into believing in the sufficiency—indeed, the moral superiority—of self-reliance. Permeating our thinking is the image of the self-made man who by hard work and, supposedly, no help from anyone else made his way to the top of the ladder and attained well-deserved respect, wealth, and independence. Such a myth is based on, and fosters, the illusion that "strong" people do not need anyone else. But even in our more modestly "independent" acts, we all depend on others, often unseen others. Going to the grocery store to choose and buy our food—or finding ourselves so "independent" that we can rely on a dietician to plan our meals, a shopper to fetch the ingredients, and a chef to prepare them for us—do we pause to consider how many people are involved in the process of making our food available? At the least, farmers, fertilizer dealers, farm implement makers, butchers, food processors, and grocery personnel are involved in this process before most of us see the finished products. How silly for us to think by simply earning a living that we "made it" without any help or that we do not need help from other people. We are not totally independent; we are dependent in millions of ways we take for granted daily.

Yet this "independence" illusion creeps into our religious thinking as well. We may acknowledge the help of God when we "make it" (how many times do you hear athletes thank God for their victories yet strangely not for their defeats); but we rarely give other people the opportunity to help us, because we think we don't, or in any case shouldn't, need any help outside our religion.

We all need to have a strong basic belief—before God and ourselves—in our worth as individuals. In fact, much of Christian theology is based on God's having placed infinite worth on each human being. That belief demands that we value ourselves. But a belief that just "me and Jesus" can face the world of "fleshly evil" is misbegotten, even though it is propounded by popular preachers of the "electronic church." It closes off countless possibilities for receiving the help God offers through other people! When one allows oneself to realize he or she is not completely independent and does not need to be—when we realize we do need other people to love us, appreciate us, and help us—we then begin to take giant leaps in the spiritual growth we experience in the context of community. We no longer fear we may explode from having bottled up our emotions, as well we might in continuing to face pain and the challenges of hope, all by ourselves.

Through sharing, we find out we are not at all "weird" for feeling such strong emotions, as we may have thought we were because no one else *seemed* to feel the way we did. Through sharing our pain with others, whether individually or in groups, we find the greatest source of hope and comfort imaginable. And from the comfort we enjoy from others' care, we experience more significant growth and healing. Such contact also gives us the perfect opportunity to discover others who are experiencing similar difficulties so that we may offer our help to them!

Help and Healing

A young couple I know very well decided to take one of their frequent evening drives in the country in the twilight of a gloriously colorful summer sunset. Only a few months before, the two had moved into a new community. They often took these country drives to get away from the frustrations and struggles of their new situation.

Things had not gone well since they had relocated. In the community from which they came, they had enjoyed many friends, the security and satisfaction of meaningful careers, an active and friendly church, the familiarity of the home they enthusiastically decorated together, and many other comforts, relationships, and benefits from having lived in this community for several years.

Yet they decided to relocate to this new community because one of them was offered a promotion and a raise in salary. Things were not as cozy or comfortable in their new city, they quickly learned. Many things they had taken for granted in their former community, things like knowing how to get to the grocery store, choosing and making appointments with doctors and dentists, getting to a bank—all these simple activities became a frustrating ordeal involving searching tiny unfamiliar maps for tiny unfamiliar streets. Everywhere they went there were strangers where before there had been friends. They found themselves incredibly lonely and very much hurt that no one knew them well enough to care or help.

In addition, the young woman's job for which they had moved turned out to be quite different from what they had expected (and by no means a positive experience). Besides all these things, the husband had resigned a fulfilling job only to find long waiting lists of job seekers ahead of him.

At times the couple's country drives were crying sessions during which they would release their feelings of loneliness, hurt, anger, and frustration. Vaguely, they hoped things would get better. Yet they couldn't understand what had happened: They had planned so well. They had gone to church and prayed about whether to accept the move. They had tried to be nice to people they encountered in their new environment; but no one, it seemed, was nice back. "Where is God?" they wondered.

As they were driving on one particularly magnificent evening, suddenly the car quit working. Stranded deep in the country, they tried to repair the car but to no avail. What else could go wrong!

Just as they were ready to begin the long walk back to town, an elderly man in a rusted truck pulled up and said, "Can I give you some help?"

"No, thanks," the young man answered, "it would be too much trouble."

With a sly smile and a chuckle, the man responded, "If it were too much trouble, I wouldn't have offered. Climb in!"

The couple reluctantly joined him, and as they were returning toward town, the man told them, "You know, I usually don't go home that way where your car was. But I just thought I would tonight."

"We're glad you did. We appreciate your help," the woman of the couple haltingly answered (since it was clear her husband was still too angry about the car to make conversation).

"Well, I'm glad when people let me help 'em. They don't all do, you know," the old man said as an aside. "Yes, ever since my wife died and people did things that showed me how much they cared—bringing over food, sending sympathy cards, stuff like that—ever since then, I decided to help somebody out whenever I could. It was people helping me through a hard time that made the difference. It's funny. I miss my wife more than anything. But in a way, I'm thankful that I finally learned how much people can care. I don't think I really knew that before."

As the man let the couple off at their home, he said, "God bless you, now!"

"God just did."

Feeling quite differently now than when they had left the

house, even with their car still stranded out in the countryside, the couple mysteriously felt made anew with hope from their encounter with the old man. It seemed as if God had visited them to say, "I am with you. I am helping you. Things will get better."

What do you suppose they would have felt like if they had walked home?

One might say this meeting was coincidence; certainly it was a meeting by chance. Does that make it any less an encouraging reminder of "no pain, no gain"?

The encounter was, I believe, the work of God's people helping one another by offering hope and support in the midst of struggle. For when we feel like we are alone and stranded in a strange, even hostile, territory, *there are plenty of God's people around who will help if we allow them to.* But allowing them to help means admitting to ourselves that we cannot solve all our problems by ourselves. We need help!

The young couple began to realize that they needed help; they couldn't face all their problems alone. Realizing that their past attitude toward new acquaintances was a friendliness more passive than active, they invited people over to their home in an effort to make new friends. They selected a church with many activities to share faith through personal contact with others. They searched for ways in which they might be of service to their new neighbors and learned that many persons in the neighborhood were also searching for friendly people with whom to associate. Most important, the couple eventually came to realize that their pain and loneliness were ways through which they perceived their needs and began to seek help. This whole process was set in motion because they reluctantly accepted help from a man who knew what it felt like to be stranded on a lonely road!

God supplies help in many more ways than we can possibly imagine or perceive. But when we learn to be sensitive to the avenues of help God offers, we open ourselves to receiving previously blocked inspiration of hope, faith, and love. For if our hurt is isolation, God comes as a welcomed friend to help share our burden. If our pain is grief over the loss of a beloved, God helps ease our hurt through the many expressions of care and concern people so marvelously give when they see a person in need. If our struggles are related to the many stresses placed on our marriage and family relationships, God's help may come through seeking and receiving the benefit of professional counseling or by bending the ear of good, caring, listening friends.

Pain is our friend when its discomfort motivates us to seek help, and not keep our difficulties to ourselves.

When pain is held inside, it intensifies and eats away at our soul like acid; but when it is openly shared, it can be wondrously lessened. Of course, sharing pain and problems is not easy. It takes a willingness to reveal, to ourselves and others, our vulnerability—and that takes courage. Just as athletes repeat the phrase "no pain, no gain," they also sometimes say, "*no guts, no glory*." Courage is not as difficult to come by when a person with whom you choose to share your pain is someone in whom you know you can confidently place your trust. Although choosing your confidants involves risk that should not be taken lightly, you may know many trustworthy persons who would be very willing to offer their help. But they cannot read your mind; you must have the courage to come forward. Your action will not only benefit you, it will benefit them, too! For most of the time we find we are never happier than when we are doing something to help someone else. And in this helpful process we all find healing.

The Wounded Healer

Probably the most significant spiritual gain we can reap from our struggles is to learn that help must flow from God through us to others, even while we feel hurt ourselves. For showing others we care is the very core of what it means to practice Christian love as it has been demonstrated to us through Jesus Christ.

One of the most spiritually sensitive persons in our world today is Henri Nouwen. Among his many insightfully written books is *The Wounded Healer*. In describing the particular difficulties of ministry in our complex contemporary world, Nouwen notes that many people in modern society suffer because they are "wounded" by a general lack of hope, by loneliness, and by an increasing "rootlessness" experienced widely within our culture. Nouwen suggests that one is a successful and effective minister to others only to the degree that one is open to experiencing personally these "wounds" of society; that only by truly feeling the hurt of the world can one understand how to help the wounded.

Nouwen's idea of the "wounded healer" is not only extremely helpful among professional clergy in their efforts to help others, it is of immense value to *all* who hurt from the painful wounds of modern struggles. For the most important feature of the wounded healer image is that it turns our primary attention away from our own hurtful wounds toward becoming a helpful "healer" of the wounds of those around us! Becoming a wounded healer carries with it tremendous responsibility: We can no longer deny or ignore our own pain, for this denial robs us of our vital ability to empathize with our brothers and sisters who also hurt. In refusing to suffer our hurts alone, we learn that many other wounded healers stand with us.

Living as a wounded healer not only increases our responsibility, it also mysteriously lessens our load.

So becoming a wounded healer, paradoxically, is a means through which we receive God's helpful healing for our own wounds, by reaching out to help God heal others. Until we break out of a preoccupation with our own pain by reaching out *from* our pain to help others, we will not fully experience the richest dimensions and meaning of spiritual growth and healing. All pain, gain, hope, help, joy, and true fulfillment are felt only within the context of our relationships with other people—community. And our community is found only in that degree to which we are willing to move beyond ourselves to consider the needs of others. Our community may be found partly in a church group, but all of us have innumerable other opportunities to share with others. The important fact is that our pain must *find* its help and *give* its help within a group of people for our spiritual growth to have its deepest meaning.

Of course, this doesn't mean blurting out every little discomfort every time you go to church or bravely "martyring" yourself by condescendingly stooping to help others. Surprisingly many persons make a career out of such "sharing" (which is really complaining and pointless egoism). We all learn to avoid asking some people how they are feeling for fear they will indeed tell us ("terrible"), just as we don't ask others because they seem unable to be honest ("everything is going great"). True wounded healers learn when it is appropriate to share and when it is most helpful to allow another the chance to receive care. When we are consistently faithful in temporarily withholding expression of our own needs in order that others may reveal theirs, we will always find that the right time will come for us to share our burdens as well.

Being a wounded healer is not a difficult process to understand—yet it is the most difficult task we will ever attempt. It may be as simple as nodding your head in affirmation of a friend's intimate sharing of his burden or as difficult as facing a long-lingering death of a much-loved family member or friend. Yet it is this paradoxical relationship between wounds and healing, life and death, pain and gain, hope and help, guts and glory, and all the rest—*it is only in allowing ourselves to feel the intensity of these seemingly opposite emotions that we find ourselves living at the very core of the life God graciously gives us*! Here the depths of life's spiritual meaning soak into our being. May our goal be to stand ever in joyous awe of the splendor of the gift of living! Here, at the core, pain and gain merge in such a way that it no longer matters so much *why* we suffer, for our attention is too intensely focused on probing the meaning of God's creation to be distracted with pain and discipline.

I must admit I have known few people who have attained such spiritual heights. I admire them as one admires the lofty achievements of a mountain climber from the safe, level plains below. Yet I will never cease to be awestruck at the knowledge that those who have scaled the highest spiritual peaks are also among those who have suffered the most pain. These persons, it seems, are like Moses, who led his people from bondage and struggled up the mountain to stand in the very presence of God. By his experience, Moses was transformed; he had lived for a moment or two in divine splendor.

One such person I have had the privilege to know was Mance Gilliam, who lived in Durham, North Carolina.

Mance

Mance was the youngest of twelve brothers and sisters born into a Southern black sharecropper's family during the earliest part of this century. It was his mother's dream that one of her children attend college.

Now, one can only imagine some of the special difficulties and struggles involved in sending a young black man, however intelligent, through college in the racial climate of the 1920s South. But although there was little money among the Gilliams, the whole family cooperated in pooling available financial resources, funneling cash downward so that the youngest member might receive the education that had long been Mance's mother's dream. Through his family's love and labors (and much hard work of his own), Mance successfully graduated and began work for the North Carolina Mutual Insurance Company, then one of the largest black-owned businesses in the nation, and advanced to the position of vice-president supervising all the company's field agents. Mance's career was highly successful and rewarding.

But he did not reserve his skills and talents for business use only. Mance was also a leader in his local church as well as within the wider world of his denomination, the African Methodist Episcopal Church, Zion. He was elected a delegate to every national general conference between 1948 and 1976. Through his extensive travels and influence in the black community throughout the South, Mance attained a position from which he assisted eight financially struggling black colleges in remaining open during the Depression years. His work with these institutions of higher learning, one of which he felt privileged to have attended, was his proudest achievement.

When I first met Mance, he had been "retired" for over ten years and had aged to his late seventies. He was working as a volunteer fund-raiser for a senior citizens agency serving mostly lower-income urban dwellers. With a spry spring in his step and an unmistakable vibrancy in his smile, he greeted each of the senior citizens every day as he came into work at the senior center. Mance volunteered an average of thirty to forty hours per week to the agency. No one who witnessed his energy and attitude could have found it easy to believe he was older than many of the residents!

In long talks together over lunch, Mance shared with me wonderful stories about many of the struggles of his life. He filled me with inspiration by communicating not just the fascinating events, but also his own profoundly perceptive spiritual interpretation of each experience. In all his struggles with racist whites seeking to bankrupt the financially fragile small Southern black colleges, Mance saw a larger spiritual battle being waged between prejudice and divine justice. In his work for the insurance company he had seen God's care for a painfully oppressed people at work, providing valuable financial protection to those who could find such security nowhere else. And in his work with the senior citizens agency, Mance saw the opportunity to serve those who had not been as fortunate as he, devoting long hours and much energy to help them out. For Mance, such efforts were not woeful duty; they were spontaneous acts of gratitude to the people he felt had helped him all his life.

In all these many activities taking place over a significant period of time, Mance had seen and faced more painful conflict than I had even imagined. And for him each event was a spiritual struggle. To Mance there was no separation between the sacred and the secular. His career, church work, and volunteerism were all one and the same: they were service to God and they were a struggle. It was his ability to face—even seek out—such painful experience in this spirit that made Mance one of the most remarkable persons I have ever known.

As a young and inexperienced student preparing for the ministry, one day I complained to Mance about some of the particular sacrifices the church expects professional ministers to make. Mance lightheartedly chuckled—and gave me some advice I would remember.

"Even though I wasn't a preacher, I once wrestled with that devil, too," he began. "One time, I remember, there was a Sunday morning when I was thinking hard about dumping the whole thing. I was tired of fighting all that mess out there," he said with a sweeping gesture seeming to suggest he was talking about the whole world of strife. "I was working with those colleges in Birmingham and Atlanta that were having a hard time and were calling on me. Oh, it was a mess. Everybody fussing and carrying on, wringing their hands over what we were going to do. I felt like I could take no more, and I'll tell you I was wrestling with the temptation to give up the fight."

Then Mance leaned over the table and opened his eyes wide and said, "But I went to church that Sunday morning anyway. And do you know what the preacher talked about? He talked about Saint Paul telling Titus to stay in Crete. You know that story how in Paul's letter to young Titus he told him to stay in Crete and preach the Word. Now Titus didn't *want* to stay there. Crete was an awful place—full of false preachers and everybody wrangling amongst themselves. But Paul said to Titus,"—Mance spoke slowly, in a whisper, as he pointed and leaned even closer—"Stay in Crete, Titus. Stay in Crete."

Then Mance sat back, suddenly relaxed, and said, "He was talking right to me, you see. It was like God was saying to me in that mess I was in, 'Mance, stay in Crete; stay in Birmingham.' When I heard those words that day, I just couldn't give up. We kept on fighting, and before long we had convinced those old Bull Conner boys in Birmingham to help us keep that school open."

But then Mance's fierce intensity returned as he again pointed and leaned forward toward me. "Son, what I'm saying to you is stay in Crete. Stay in Crete. I know it's a mess and a struggle. But stay in Crete!"

I will never forget the way he looked at me as he said those words. I once heard someone say, "If you haven't seen God in the eyes of another human being, you haven't seen God!" That day one could not help but see God in the eyes of Mance. And hearing those words "Stay in Crete!" had much the same effect on me as "No pain, no gain!" directed toward me much later by my jogging partner. In both cases those were words of help from God, encouraging me in my spiritual struggle to continue on a little further so that I might learn and grow.

Less than two weeks after delivering his inspiring speech to me, Mance was hospitalized. After only a few more days, he died. I learned that for several years Mance had known he was terminally ill with cancer. He had chosen to tell this news only to his closest friends and a very few church members, because he wanted to keep on working and helping people.

Months later while recalling his "stay in Crete" admonition, I thought of how Mance himself lived its essence to the very end. Even while bearing the deep wounds and battle scars left from a life full of strife (and while others might have thought he could simply "throw in the towel," already having done more than his part), in an astounding display of spiritual maturity, he spent his last days helping to heal the hurts of others. He was working for the comfort of others even in his own great discomfort.

Such lofty heights of spiritual growth not many of us can scale. Yet the spiritual truth of Mance Gilliam's experience applies to us all: Through his pain from working to relieve the difficulties and suffering of others, Mance embraced the burden and the joy of finding that pain and gain do journey together in life. Surely he inspired many others to emulate his healing example.

The philosopher and psychologist William James once said, "The greatest use of a life is to spend it on something that outlasts it." Mance Gilliam demonstrated to me that nothing outlasts the influence of spiritual growth learned through struggle, discipline, and pain.

POSTSCRIPT

The world breaks everyone and afterward many are
strong at the broken places.
—Ernest Hemingway

After looking more closely at pain and gain, we still cannot
explain the "curious paradox." Even more troublesome is the
fact that our world contains millions of people keenly aware
that they experience *much* pain and *no* gain. The agonizing
words of Jesus—"Why?"—will continue to echo in the hearts
not only of all who must struggle with personal pain but also
for those who must witness the tremendous amount of innocent and senseless suffering all too easily found around the
globe.

So the path of spiritual growth turns us ultimately toward
a more global perspective on our problems. For in the midst
of the trials we experience personally, it may be helpful to
ponder the old Byzantine proverb recalled by Don Paarlberg,
former assistant secretary of agriculture and a specialist in
world hunger, in his book *Farmers of Five Continents*:

> He who has bread has many problems.
> He who lacks bread has only one problem.

If our own pain and discipline remind us of our personal dependence upon God, the large-scale suffering from the "one problem" we witness in our world challenges us to deepen our commitment toward alleviating life's most crucial problems. Indeed, the same principles of pain and growth are applicable to the problems facing our nations: we must grapple with these difficulties and grow toward meaningful solutions if we are to survive. It is and will continue to be a struggle.

Yet we learn, as M. Scott Peck put it, "Life is difficult." And "Once we truly know that life is difficult—once we truly understand and accept it—then life is no longer difficult. Because once it is accepted, the fact that life is difficult no longer matters." When we accept that pain and discipline are an integral part of spiritual growth, personally and globally, we then learn to focus on continuing growth not present hurts.

This gives us hope to keep trying and dreaming. It is dreaming of this hopeful day that Mary Ann Bernard has expressed in her poem "Resurrection."

Long, long, long ago;
Way before this winter's snow
First fell upon these weathered fields;
I used to sit and watch and feel
And dream of how the spring would be,
When through the winter's stormy sea
She'd raise her green and growing head,
Her warmth would resurrect the dead.

Long before this winter's snow
I dreamt of this day's sunny glow
And thought somehow my pain would pass
With winter's pain, and peace like grass
Would simply grow. The pain's not gone.
It's still as cold and hard and long
As lonely pain has ever been,
It cuts so deep and far within.

Long before this winter's snow
I ran from pain, looked high and low
For some fast way to get around
Its hurt and cold. I'd have found,
If I had looked at what was there,
That things don't follow fast or fair.
That life goes on, and times do change,
And grass does grow despite life's pains.

Long before this winter's snow
I thought that this day's sunny glow,
The smiling children and growing things
And flowers bright were brought by spring.
Now, I know the sun does shine,
That children smile, and from the dark, cold, grime
A flower comes. It groans, yet sings,
And through its pain, its peace begins.

Mary Ann Bernard

BRUISED BUT NOT BROKEN

STANLEY C. BALDWIN

CARMEL • NEW YORK 10512

Cover design and illustration by Al Mendenhall
Edited by Steve Halliday

BRUISED BUT NOT BROKEN
© 1985 by Multnomah Press
Portland, Oregon 97266

Printed in the United States of America

This Guideposts edition is published by
special arrangement with Multnomah Press.

Library of Congress Cataloging in Publication Data

Baldwin, Stanley C.
    Bruised but not broken.

    1. Christian life—1960-   2. Consolation.
I. Title.
BV4501.2.B3818   1985   248.4   85-2977

         87 88 89 90 91 – 10 9 8 7 6 5 4 3 2

Contents

Foreword

This is a wonderful book. After all the "how-to" and "can-do" volumes that have been filling the shelves of Christian bookstores, it is a relief to read someone who can identify with our real situations and tell it the way it is. Stanley Baldwin is a friend who talks with us in nontechnical ways about the things that matter most to us—the things that keep us from the Christian victory stand. As he says, the real reason that the Christian rejoices is not that he has come through triumphantly, but that God is always with us to strengthen us.

The incidents and illustrations here related are taken from real life. People are frustrated; people fail; people become victims of illness; people die. Yet God is there, and that's what we want to hear. That's the encouragement we need.

Miracles are dandy, but God is better. He won't let us down.

Mr. Baldwin is a Christian writer who helps people. The hard places will still be there after you have read this book. But you will have the joy of this assurance: you are not alone. That's not much of a cushion, but it is a great lift to the morale. And it is morale—not aspirin—that wins the battles of life, morale that is solidly based on the fruit of the Spirit.

Recently I was in a prayer meeting and discovered that two of those present were afraid to go home that night. Dig underneath the pleasant smiles of most folks and you will find deep, deep hurts. For all such, a thoughtful perusal of these chapters will spell recognition, identity, and genuine appreciation. My congratulations to both author and publisher.

Sherwood Eliot Wirt

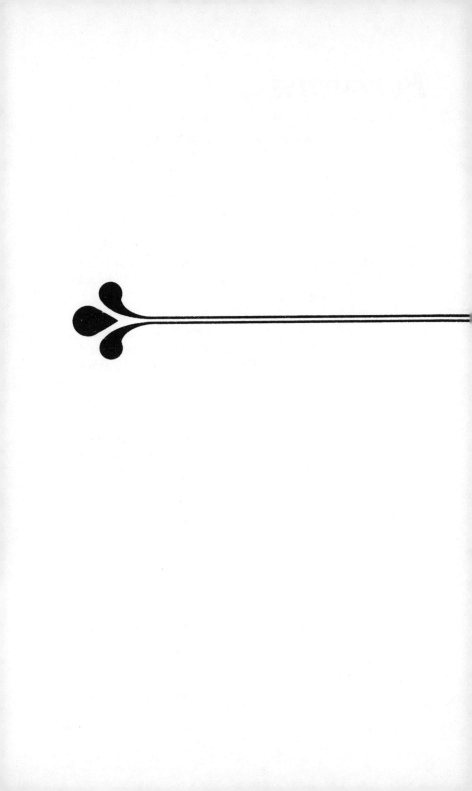

Part 1

Getting Squared
Away with God Again

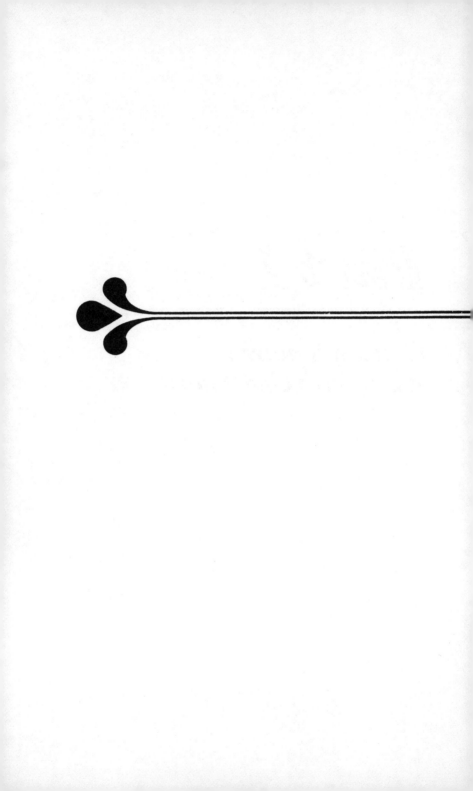

1
When It Seems God Has Failed You

A Promising Ministry

Robert Foster and his wife Jane had been called to a small, struggling church. It was Bob's first pastorate. The church could only offer a small salary, well below what the government called the poverty level. Of course, as the church grew, so would Bob's salary. In the meantime, he and Jane would have to "trust the Lord."

After much prayer, the Fosters accepted the call. They believed they were stepping out on the promise of God. One verse especially summed it up: "My God will meet all your needs according to his glorious riches in Christ Jesus" (Philippians 4:19).

Bob launched into his new ministry enthusiastically. The people were responsive and their numbers began to grow.

Then the mill—the town's chief economic support—began cutting back. One of Bob's best men was laid off and announced plans to move away.

Bob and Jane winced, but held on; they had come by faith and were not about to give up. Still, there were bills to pay, a car to keep running and insured, two small children who needed food, clothing, vitamins, doctor's visits, and maybe an occasional trip to McDonald's.

Six months later Bob and Jane looked back on those hard times as "the good old days." The mill curtailment that everyone hoped would be short-lived was shorter than anyone wanted. Now the mill would close altogether.

The church no longer had the resources to support a full-time pastor and his family. Bob and Jane were beaten. They would have to leave.

"It took us several years to get over that," they said recently. "Not just the trauma of being poor. Worse than that was the blow to our faith. We had counted on what we thought was God's promise, and we had been let down. How could we ever again be sure of his promises?"

Disappointed Faith

Like Bob and Jane, many Christians have somehow had their faith disappointed. This experience should be distinguished from merely facing difficulty or suffering. Hard as that may be, it should not be unexpected. Jesus told us that in this world we would have tribulation (see John 16:33). What's harder is to believe that God has promised us something . . . and then he fails to come through.

Disappointments to faith can occur in many different settings. Consider a few more actual cases.

The Child Who Strays

Esther is sure her little boy Eric will grow up to know and love the Lord. She claims God's promise, "Train a child in the way he should go, and when he is old he will not turn from it" (Proverbs 22:6).

Esther has been through one unsuccessful marriage and a divorce, but that was before she knew the Lord. Now middle-aged, she is an ardent Christian. Eric is the only child of her second marriage. Esther is determined that things will turn out right with Eric. She has claimed him for God.

Sue, Esther's cousin of about the same age, has been a pastor's wife for years. She tells Esther that her son will ultimately make his own choice about following the Lord. No matter what Esther does, it's possible that Eric may turn away from God. Sue has seen things like that happen. She is concerned that Esther's own faith may collapse if or when Eric strays. Not that she'd be likely to renounce Christ; but she might well join the ranks of the walking wounded and alienate herself from her Lord.

Esther doesn't come right out and say so, but she suggests that those parents whose children have strayed from God must have failed somewhere along the line. Sue admits it. Of course they have failed, all parents do. Nevertheless, Sue insists that even good parents who train their children "in the way they should go" sometimes experience heartbreak as they see their children turn from God.

Esther remains unshaken. She has God's promise. "God said it, I believe it, and that settles it," she declares.

But life has a way of "unsettling" things. In this case it remains to be seen whether Esther is right. But there certainly are some parents who once echoed her convictions, only to find out the hard way that they were wrong.

The Healing That Never Comes

A hundred miles away from where Esther is claiming her son for God, a woman named Francine also claimed a divine promise.

Francine was a delightful, warm-hearted woman, aged thirty-nine. She loved the Lord and she loved people. She was the spiritual sparkplug of her family. Though her husband and three almost-grown children were Christians, it was Francine who glowed for God.

Even after grim-faced doctors diagnosed her "gall bladder problem" as liver cancer and gave her ten weeks to live, Francine remained positive. She believed in the healing power of God. Far more than affirming that God *could* heal her, Francine believed he *would*.

As she prayed and studied the scriptural promises, Francine became even more certain of her healing. For her to die made no sense. Her family needed her. She was a key witness for Christ in a dark community. She was still young. Surely this sickness was an attack of Satan.

Francine got some teaching tapes that encouraged her to "name it and claim it." Whatever she would ask in Jesus' name, believing, it would be granted. The Word of God said so (see Matthew 21:22; John 14:13).

The ten weeks allotted by her doctors came and went with Francine still very much alive. She reported at a church service that she'd had a vision from the Lord. In the vision she had seen herself completely healed.

So despite the yellow color of her skin that betrayed a diseased liver, Francine kept "naming and claiming" her healing.

Then about eighteen months after she became ill, Francine noticed one day that her stools had turned white. She knew what that meant—the disease had proceeded to the point of no return. Her liver damage was irreversible. She could not live.

Francine wept out her fear and disappointment to a close friend, but then resumed her "naming and claiming." There were preparations for death that Francine needed to make, but couldn't, because she was "going to be healed." Her family, following her example, treated her almost as if she were not sick. Longstanding problems between Francine and her children continued unresolved just as they had for years.

Toward the end, she became too weak to deal with the questions *why?* and *what happened to God's promise?*

About two years after she became ill, Francine died.
Her husband and children haven't been to church since.

The Equal Yoke that Breaks

Michelle is a young mother of four children. Her first husband walked out on her four years ago. Since then, Michelle has come to know the Lord and has found a whole new life in Christ.

Like most other single parents, Michelle entertained hopes of one day marrying again. Her church taught that as the innocent party, Michelle was free to remarry, only "in the Lord." That meant she should definitely marry a man who shared her faith in Christ. It also meant that she needed to marry in God's will.

"We know it's hard to wait, but God will bless you for it," her friends said.

Michelle had made a firm commitment to Christ as Lord and wasn't about to compromise that now by marrying unwisely. She gave the whole matter to the Lord in prayer.

Two years later Michelle walked down the aisle, her heart almost bursting with joy. She had honored the Lord, and now he had given her a Christian man with whom to share the rest of her life.

Today Michelle is alone again with her four children. She lives on welfare.

Her husband walked out on her.

The Search for Answers

What can we say to these things? How shall we help those who have been disappointed when they acted on their faith in God's promises? Are the promises of God to be trusted?

Let's consider some answers often suggested. Perhaps each one is at least partially correct.

1. *The promises don't fail, people do.*

Perhaps the most common reaction Christians have to another's disappointed faith is suspicion (or even accusation). "Let God be true, and every man a liar" expresses this view (see Romans 3:4). If your faith was disappointed, you must have failed to meet the conditions; that's all there is to it. If a child goes astray, he wasn't truly trained up in the way he should go. If a pastor was driven out by lack of funds, he must have given up too easily, lacked faith, or failed somehow. If a sick person was not healed, he must have lacked faith or misinterpreted the promises in the first place. If a woman's marriage fails twice, she must harbor some grievous fault.

Maybe so. Sometimes people do fail God and then blame him for failing them. But to say that is true in a specific case can be both judgmental and cruel. It places us in the company of Job's accusers. They were sure Job was responsible somehow for the calamities that befell him. In their view, either God or Job was at fault. Since they were not about to blame God, that left Job as the only candidate.

They were wrong.

2. *The promises are "spiritual," not literal.*

With a little imagination almost all of God's promises can be explained away. Does the Bible say, "My God shall supply all your needs"? (Philippians 4:19, NASB). Yes, but what does a Christian really need? We don't need anything, some say, except Jesus. We don't need money, cars, houses, lands, food, health. We don't even need to survive here on earth. We have all in Jesus.

One preacher went so far as to claim that this is why the verse (in many versions) says God will supply your *need* rather than your *needs;* your only need is Jesus.

The many promises that prayer will be answered can be dealt with handily by a similar spiritualizing. People pray for a sick person to get well; they claim the relevant promises. Then when the patient dies someone says, "He has received his perfect healing. He has gone to be with the Lord, where there is no more sickness or pain."

If it's prosperity that is promised, one can say, "Well, we may be poor in this world's goods, but we are rich in heavenly things."

This approach is not wholly wrong. No doubt some have "claimed" promises that God never made, or they have misunderstood and misapplied a legitimate one. We parents should understand this well, because our own children often read into our remarks ironclad promises that we never intended.

"Can we go to the beach next Saturday? Please, Mommy?"

"Well, maybe, if it's a nice day."

Saturday dawns bright and clear, and before Mommy is even wide awake the child is excitedly preparing to go to the beach.

"We *can't* go, dear," Mommy explains. "The car's broken down."

"But you promised! Waaaah."

It's possible to read into another's words more than was intended. Is it possible we sometimes do that with God?

On the other hand, explaining away God's promises in this fashion can also be a cop-out. When Paul said that God would supply all our need, did he mean that our only need is Jesus? No! The context speaks about material needs. The Christians at Philippi sent a gift to Paul out of concern for him, and in return Paul wanted to assure them that God would provide for their needs as well.

Maybe some promises are to be taken "spiritually," but we also need to remember the old maxim: "Those who have spiritual eyes don't spiritualize and thereby tell spiritual lies."

3. *The "promises" are general statements of fact or are*

specific promises to others; they are not necessarily personal guarantees to us.

"Train a child in the way he should go, and when he is old he will not turn from it." This is no guarantee from God that your child, if he is trained properly in the Christian faith, will be a Christian. It is rather a general observation about the nature of life. Childhood training will ordinarily have a lasting and decisive effect on a person.

Some point out that the saying is, after all, a proverb, and is identified as such in the text (see Proverbs 10:1). It is a saying much like, "A rolling stone gathers no moss," or "A stitch in time saves nine." Should you happen to find moss on a rolling stone, you would not therefore enter a crisis of faith, reject the proverb's validity, and doubt the integrity of the one who spoke it. Should a stitch in time prove wasted on occasion because the whole fabric is rotten, that would not invalidate the proverb.

Other promises, one might argue, are like the assurance Paul gave the Philippians that their needs would be supplied. This was addressed to them, not to us.

While there is validity to the argument that not everything in the Bible applies directly to us, we'd lose virtually the whole book if we never acted on anything originally addressed to someone else.

So how do we decide whether a biblical promise is ours to claim personally and literally? That's a tough question. We don't want to be among those who do not have because we do not ask. But neither do we want to end up doubting God—or secretly angry at him—because we have assumed too much.

My own answer is that if a humble study of the Scriptures plus the inner witness of the Spirit leads me to believe a promise is for me, then I claim it. But even when I do so, I try to *center my faith supremely in the Promiser rather than in the promise.* There is a difference!

Faith in Formulas

Something about human nature loves formulas. We want predictability, regularity, uniformity. This desire isn't bad. There is order in the universe. Science would be impossible if everything behaved randomly, if there were no "promise" that a given set of conditions would produce a given result.

Our trouble is that we sometimes try to put God in our little boxes. We want predictable, regular, and uniform behavior from him. Within very large parameters, even this is okay. God is love and we must expect that he will predictably, regularly, and uniformly act on the basis of love.

But that doesn't mean we can predict what specific action he will take in a given case. Paul knew that: "O the depth of the riches both of the wisdom and knowledge of God! how unsearchable are His judgments, and His ways past finding out!" (Romans 11:33, KJV).

Though God's ways are "past finding out," we continue to imagine that we have found them out. Based on this arrogant assumption, we proceed to predict what God will do—and sometimes what he *must* do. If he fails to salute sometime when we raise our flag, suddenly there's a crisis.

It seems that we want God to put his omnipotence to work in our situation, but we don't want his omniscience—we think we already know enough ourselves.

Job found that God didn't always act according to his expectations, nor according to those of his contemporaries. Still he was able to say, "Though he slay me, yet will I hope in him" (Job 13:15). He could no longer say, "I trust this or that will be the outcome," but he could still say, "I trust in him."

There is a song I used to take exception to every time I heard it. The song expressed a strong determination to go on believing in God no matter what. It said something to the effect that even if the sun and moon stopped shining and no miracle were ever seen again, the singer would still trust in the Lord.

I thought, *No, that sounds good, but it's an exaggeration. If the sun and moon ceased to shine, that would prove God untrue, because he said they would shine until the end of time* (see Genesis 8:22).

Now I've decided the song is right. It still sounds like an implicit contradiction of Scripture, and I fully expect to see both the sun and the moon shining until Jesus comes. But if they don't, I'll still believe. My faith is in God, not in some conditions I understand him to have promised.

Celebrating God

Many martyrs have given their lives for the cause of Christ, and reading of them is no particular test of faith for most believers. We don't wrestle with questions about how God could have allowed it. Jesus forewarned his followers to expect persecution. We are not surprised at anything the world might do to Christians.

One particular incident, however, seems disturbingly different. These men died, not at the hands of an enemy, but because "God let them starve."

Perhaps I'm especially fascinated with Captain Allen Gardiner because the last dramatic chapter of his life began on my birthday, December 17. It was on that date, though back in 1850, that Gardiner and six intrepid companions landed at Patagonia on the southern tip of South America. Their task was to take the gospel to a people so primitive that the evolutionist Charles Darwin had said they existed "in a lower state . . . than in any other part of the world."

Gardiner, a seasoned captain of the British navy, had made careful preparations for their mission. He had twice before visited the area, once staying for three months. He knew the natives to be treacherous cannibals and the land and weather to be severe.

He took with him two double-deck launches, the *Pioneer* and the *Speedwell,* and six-months' supply of provisions. His team included a medical doctor and a ship's carpenter. In England he had a group of supporters who were to send him a second six-months' supply of goods.

On December 18 Gardiner said goodbye to the *Ocean Queen,* the ship that had carried his party from England. "Nothing can exceed the cheerful endurance and unanimity of the whole party," he wrote. "I feel that the Lord is with us, and cannot doubt that he will own and bless the work which he has permitted us to begin."

The very next month Gardiner's supporters in England began seeking a ship to carry the next six-months' provisions to Patagonia. No one would risk it. Can you imagine the thoughts of the missionaries as day after day they searched the horizon for a ship that never came? Could the tempter have passed up such an opportunity to question the love and faithfulness of Almighty God?

Fighting scurvy, cold, and hunger, plus the hostility of those they had come to win, the little band must have known some dark days of discouragement.

In October of 1851, when a relief ship finally reached Patagonia, the horrified crew found the missionaries dead of starvation. Gardiner's body, clad in three suits and with wool stockings over his arms to ward off the numbing cold, was found lying beside a boat. In his journal was a record of the ordeal. At one point Gardiner wrote:

> Poor and weak as we are, our boat is very
> Bethel to our souls, for we feel and know
> that God is here. Asleep or awake, I am,
> beyond the power of expression, happy.

God did not supply his physical needs. He and his companions had sought first the kingdom of God, but the material things had not been added unto them. Still, while he could not say God's provision was there, he could and did say, "God is here."

I do not know whether Captain Gardiner or his men ever wondered if God had failed them. If they did, there was no hint of it in his last communication. It was dated September 6, 1851, almost nine months after his arrival in Patagonia and only about a month before help arrived.

> Yet a little while and though . . . (obliterated) the Almighty to sing the praises . . . throne. I neither hunger nor thirst, though five days without food . . .

Eight years later the society Gardiner had founded sent a second mission to Patagonia. The natives attacked, killing all but one of the party.

Two years after that a third effort resulted in a permanent station, and after four years more, the first baptisms. Eventually a boat was commissioned to work all along the coast, taking the gospel to the natives; its name, the *Allen Gardiner*.

At last even Charles Darwin acknowledged his admiration for the results. "The success of the mission," he wrote, "is most wonderful and charms me, as I always prophesied utter failure. I shall feel proud if your committee think fit to elect me an honorary member of your society."

Can we trust God to keep his promises?

We cannot be sure God will always do what we think he should. David wrote, "I was young and now I am old, yet I have never seen the righteous forsaken or their children begging bread" (Psalm 37:25). But David never knew Allen Gardiner, did he?

Nevertheless, God does take care of his own. If in his divine wisdom he sees fit to make an exception to some general rule, we should say, "Let God be God."

Yes, we can trust God to keep his promises. More than that, *we can trust God*.

He is the King of the universe, the all-knowing

Sovereign, the Almighty. He has said he loves us . . . and he sent his only Son to prove it.

And *that* is a God to be trusted!

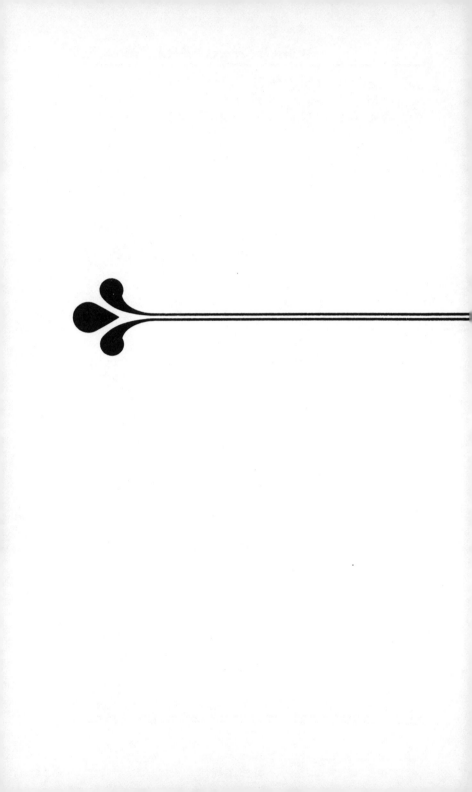

2
When You Know You Have Failed God

205 Pounds Of Guilt

Betty Hunt had finally reached the end. Not the bottom—she had been there a long time. Almost all her life. As a child she was ashamed of herself, of her poor parents, of her clothes, of wetting her pants, of being fat, of having no friends.

There had been hope briefly in her teens. A foster family had taken her to church and she had responded to the message of salvation through Christ. To get love, she could accept even the strict standards of the home—including no shows and no dances. But when she felt unaccepted there, when she knew she was still second-rate, she turned from God.

She married early—a man whose parents thought she wasn't good enough for their son. She proved them right. While he was away in the navy, she had affairs with other men. After they divorced, she left him with both of their children so she would not have the responsibility. Not that she would give up her fast life of drink and men to take care of them anyhow; but this was simpler.

Betty spent the next years as a promiscuous drunk in

a life of hell on earth. She drank so she wouldn't have to think about what a rotten person she was. And she used men both to feel loved and to hurt the men.

Her daughter, at age thirteen, came back into Betty's life. Unwanted by her father, the girl had idolized her absent mother and moved in adoring her. Within a month Betty had turned her into a scared, angry, bitter girl ready for the streets.

By this time Betty had been "dried out" at every hospital in the city and owed so many bills that neither the hospitals nor the ambulance companies would serve her anymore. They had given up on her and told her so. "If you want to kill yourself, we can't stop you," they said.

Betty had been in state hospitals for the cure. She had been in Alcoholics Anonymous and had stayed dry for one year. Several times she had tried to kill herself with an overdose of drugs and alcohol. She had been in a coma once for twenty-seven hours, and the doctors had predicted she would die or become a vegetable.

Now at age thirty-eight she was at the end. She couldn't drink any more and live, but she couldn't stop, either. She got on her knees. "God, I can't take it anymore," she prayed.

That was four years ago, and Betty Hunt hasn't had a drink since. "God gave me sobriety," she says. "There is no other explanation. I didn't imagine it would be easy and it wasn't. But I felt I had a promise from the Lord and he would always be there and that together we could make it."

The desire to die left Betty immediately. Before, she had been terrified of death, even though she didn't want to live. She felt unworthy of life, and that was one reason she drank. Now she began overcoming a lifelong weight problem also, going from 205 pounds to 125.

Other remarkable things began to happen. Before, she had been a people-pleaser, trying to be what others wanted so they would accept her. At the same time, she had been a people-hater, deliberately hurting others out of her own pain and anger.

Now God began showing her how destructive all of this was. She could not be what others wanted—and she didn't need to be. She could only be who she was. She didn't have to hurt others, either.

God also turned her guilt around. She'd had plenty of guilt, and she drank so as not to feel it. Now God had forgiven her. Christ had died for all her sins. She felt pain over what she had done, especially as she saw the effects in her daughter and son. Sometimes the guilt would threaten to come surging back. Betty knew she couldn't allow it to engulf her, or it would send her right back to drink. All she could do was live responsibly toward her daughter and son and everyone else from now on.

So here was another paradox. Feeling guilty over all her wrongdoing only made her do worse, while feeling forgiven made her do better. That's a principle many people have yet to understand, but it's a consistent message of the Bible.

Let's consider, then, what it means to fail God, and what the Bible says to those of us who have done so.

I've Let God Down

Richard Nixon lost the presidency of the United States over Watergate. He was the only president in history to resign the office. Had he not done so, he almost certainly would have been impeached.

For years afterward, Nixon was asked why he would not—then or since—simply confess his wrong and ask the forgiveness of the American people. His response was that he would not grovel.

The former president did, however, confess with apparent pain that he had "let down" his family, his friends and supporters, and the American people. It obviously hurt him to feel and know that he had so grievously failed those who had trusted him.

One of the most devastating things that can happen to any of us is to feel and know that we have let down God. Strong men weep over it. The cries of such people are among the most heart-wrenching words in Scripture.

One strong man especially comes to mind.

Peter told the Lord that he would never let him down, not even if he had to die for him. Soon afterward, he denied three times that he was a disciple of Jesus. We read that "The Lord turned and looked straight at Peter. Then Peter remembered the word the Lord had spoken to him: 'Before the rooster crows today, you will disown me three times.' And he went outside and wept bitterly" (Luke 22:61-62).

Failing the Lord was too much for him to bear.

Trouble from Within

Until now in this book we have considered things that come into our lives from outside to trouble us. Severe trials, great losses, and disappointed faith may make our very survival seem doubtful. But when we look to Christ who indwells us, we are sufficient for all these things.

A totally different sort of hard time, however, can arise from within us. For many reasons we can become deeply dissatisfied with ourselves. Maybe we abuse our children or fail them in other ways. Perhaps we get caught in criminal behavior. Or we become involved in personal scandal. Maybe, like Peter, we pledge that we will follow Christ anywhere but then fail or dishonor him.

Not only did Peter know what that was like, but it appears from Romans 7 that Paul did, too. He wrote, "I have the desire to do what is good, but I cannot carry it out. For what I do is not the good I want to do; no, the evil I do not want to do—this I keep on doing. . . . What a wretched man I am! Who will rescue me from this body of death?" (Romans 7:18, 19, 24).

Isaiah also stands out as one who knew the agonies of self-reproach. On one occasion he said, "Woe to me! I am ruined! For I am a man of unclean lips, and I live among a people of unclean lips, and my eyes have seen the King, the LORD Almighty" (Isaiah 6:5).

If you have ever felt miserable, worthless, and wretched because you somehow let down God, you know what a crushing experience it is. Yet the very persons we have observed as scriptural examples of self-loathing ought to encourage us. Who were these people who felt so worthless before God? Peter, Paul, Isaiah—hardly a list of losers. These are among the noblest names in all of history.

The miserable failures of these saints could very well have had much to do with their subsequent godly lives. By nature we are all flawed, fallen creatures, and until we're convinced of that at a gut level, we are ill-prepared to serve God. We tend to trust our own strength, not his, and to usurp the glory that belongs to him alone.

One would think that every Christian would know better—would understand his own inadequacy. We all come to Christ initially as sinners, totally dependent on the mercy of God for salvation. Nevertheless, we often drift back into the illusion that we are pretty good people.

The evidence that we are living in illusion comes when we fail the Lord *and then are surprised*. Why are we surprised? Didn't we originally sign on as sinners?

While a clear grasp of our own sinful inadequacy is necessary to spiritual maturity and usefulness, that is by no means the whole picture. God's dealing with his people never stops at the point of self-reproach.

The Worst of Sinners

Let's consider more closely the story of one man who failed God. Saul of Tarsus was a man of strong convictions

—and proud of it. Others *said* they believed, but he put shoe leather to it. Saul served the God of his fathers with great zeal.

There was the case of the "Way" sect, for example. Troublesome bunch, and persistent. Their leader had been put to death almost two years before. More recently, Saul helped organize the execution of Stephen, a spokesman for the cult. What a firebrand that man was! Tragic that he was caught up in error; he could have been such a force for God with all that zeal and conviction. Indeed, Stephen was not unlike Saul himself in that regard.

Such a destructive heresy as the "Way" had to be stopped. Saul owed that much to other promising young men like Stephen who might be sucked into this thing. And he owed it to God.

It was fortunate that the people were beginning to understand and to help obliterate the "Way." The effort to free Jerusalem of their presence had been almost totally successful. Damascus still had a nest of the cultists, though, and Saul must deal with them next.

He set out for Damascus armed with authority to arrest any "Way" adherents he might find. But between Jerusalem and Damascus, something happened to Saul. He was struck blind by a bright light, and at the same time thrown into stark confusion by a voice from heaven claiming to be Jesus, the executed leader of the "Way."

Blind and dazed, Saul spent the next three days doing some heavy thinking. Only God could speak from heaven like that, but the voice had identified itself as Jesus. Could Jesus really be God? Had Saul been fighting against God at the very time he was trying hardest to serve him? The possibilities were incredible and frightening.

Saul was still sightless, still without food, still struggling with the implications of everything that had happened to him when a visitor arrived. Ananias said Jesus had sent him—and incredibly, he knew all about Saul's odd experience on the road.

It was the final confirmation of what Saul now knew in his heart. Jesus was Messiah. The "Way" was God's way. And he, Saul, had done everything in his power to destroy the work of God.

Can you imagine what that knowledge did to a man proud of his service to God? To miss that far! To fail God so miserably! To have killed God's witnesses!

Ananias assured Saul that God would both forgive and use him. Saul immediately regained his sight, was baptized, and began to preach Christ. But he never forgot the sense of shame he felt over the abysmal way he had sinned against God. Almost twenty-five years later he told the Corinthian believers, "I am the least of the apostles and do not even deserve to be called an apostle, because I persecuted the church of God" (1 Corinthians 15:9).

Thirty years after his conversion, at the twilight of his life, he told Timothy that "Christ Jesus came into the world to save sinners—of whom I am the worst" (1 Timothy 1:15).

Self-Hate Can Kill

Seeing yourself as the worst of sinners can be fatal. More than one person, unable to cope with a sense of utter failure and worthlessness, has acted as his own judge, jury, and executioner. Others, like Betty Hunt, have killed themselves gradually with alcohol or drugs.

In *A True View of You*[1] I tell the true story of a ten-year-old boy who was so often and so strongly condemned by his mother that he hanged himself. His older sister had tried to intervene. Just before the hanging, she had told him, "It doesn't matter what she says, Rob. You're not that bad."

"Yes, I am," he said. "She's right. I'm no good. I can't do anything right. I shouldn't even be living."

Later that same day his sister found Rob hanging in a tree near their home and just managed to save his life.

Do you feel like such a failure before God that you shouldn't even be living? If so, you are overreacting. To see your own sinfulness and failure is okay. As we've said, many great Bible saints had that experience. If that's what is happening to you, congratulations! You finally see yourself as you are, with no flattering delusions.

But don't kill yourself. There is something else crucial for you to consider besides your own unworthiness. As Paul—the former "worst of sinners" Saul of Tarsus—put it, "Christ Jesus came into the world to save sinners" (1 Timothy 1:15). Or as Jesus himself said, "God did not send his Son into the world to condemn the world, but to save the world through him. Whoever believes in him is not condemned, but whoever does not believe stands condemned already" (John 3:17-18).

When you see yourself as unfit to live, you are right in one sense. But you must also see God as he is. He delights in mercy, forgiveness, new hope. "'As surely as I live,' declares the Sovereign LORD, 'I take no pleasure in the death of the wicked, but rather that they turn from their ways and live'" (Ezekiel 33:11).

The fact that you are alive means that in God's view you ought to be alive, for he could end your life at any time of his choice.

Each of us may view himself or herself in one of three ways. First, we may accept ourselves on the assumption that we are acceptable. By whatever standards we apply—with or without reference to God—we judge that we are okay, or at least fit to live. That was how Saul saw himself until his abrupt awakening. By contrast, Betty Hunt never did see herself that way.

Second, we may reject ourselves and judge that we are worthless as Betty and Rob did. But who can live with that?

Third, we may say, "I am a washout, a failure in my-self, but God in his great mercy and love has forgiven me and will make something worthwhile out of me yet."

It is this third view that transformed Saul the persecutor into Paul the apostle. It is this view that changed Betty Hunt from promiscuous drunk to responsible and loving mother. It is this view that has worked a similar transformation in millions of others.

They were unprofitable, but became profitable. They were a liability to their world, but became an asset. They were a curse, but became a blessing. They were unfit to live, but became fit to live with God forever.

NOTES

1. Stanley C. Baldwin, *A True View of You* (Ventura, Calif.: Regal Books, 1982), pp. 79-81.

3
When Forgiveness Seems Far Away

The End of the Conflict

We haven't quite told the story about Paul and his struggle with a sense of sinful worthlessness. The problem was not resolved for all time when he came to know Christ. Maybe it should have been, but it wasn't.

So far as we know, Paul never doubted that God had forgiven him for his career as a persecutor of the church. He didn't go around being tormented about what he had done "before Christ," although he did recall those days with shame. Paul did almost self-destruct over another issue, however. He grew to hate himself for his sorry performance as a Christian.

Paul never reveals the details, but the sin that got to him was covetousness. Was it for money he lusted? For the good life he saw others enjoying? For ease? For prestige? For power? For reputation among the believers?

Maybe it was all of these, for he wrote, "But sin . . . produced in me every kind of covetous desire" (Romans 7:8).

To see this rampant in himself was a crushing experience for Paul. Even in his pre-Christian days he would have disdained such sin. He had been "in regard to the law, a Pharisee . . . as for legalistic righteousness, faultless" (Philippians 3:5-6)

When he came to know Christ, his righteousness became an inner matter of the heart instead of mere outward conformity to law. Therefore, Paul expected that he would be more righteous than before, certainly not less. Now he found the crude and vulgar sin of covetousness not only present in his life, but irresistible.

It threw him into a second crisis of self-hate. "What a wretched man I am!" he cried (Romans 7:24).

Facing Hard Facts

We think it shocking when someone who claims to be a Christian behaves reprehensibly. We wonder whether such a person is truly born again. We think that if the person is a true Christian, he or she is certainly not a very good one. Sometimes we ourselves are the "someone" who sins, and we are shocked at the shattered image of our presumed godliness.

That's hard to face.

Paul faced it and drew a conclusion from it. He didn't decide that Christ was no Savior after all. He didn't dismiss as invalid his own conversion experience. Far from it. He declared. "If I do what I do not want to do, it is no longer I who do it, but it is sin living in me that does it. . . . in my inner being I delight in God's law" (Romans 7:20, 22).

Paul exonerated himself. Or rather, he came to understand that he had been exonerated. Completely.

The bottom line for Paul was not self-hate. It was not, "Oh, how holy God is and how rotten I am!" Instead, it was "There is now no condemnation for those who are in Christ Jesus," and nothing "in all creation will be able to separate us from the love of God that is in Christ Jesus our Lord" (Romans 8:1, 39).

Nothing can separate us. It is true that great psychological and emotional forces will continue to create barriers and even conflict between us and God. But Scripture likens the believer's union with the Lord to the marriage bond that makes "one flesh" out of two people. We read, "But he who unites himself with the Lord is one with him in spirit" (1 Corinthians 6:17). That is why we should not accept the thinking of those who set forth self-loathing as a standard for Christians—essentially they tear apart what God has joined together.

Let me explain what I mean.

God As Intimidator

One writer[1] who cites Isaiah's "woe-is-me" speech (chapter 2) says, "We ought to be shaken to our roots when we see ourselves in comparison to him. If we are not deeply pained about our sin, we do not understand God's holiness." A bit later, he says, "And our sense of sinfulness and fear is proportional to our experience of the presence of God."

This would all be well and good if it were portrayed as an abiding insight or an experience preparatory to salvation. But to hold up the experience as normative Christianity is neither edifying nor true. The implication is that the more we know God, the worse we should feel about ourselves.

But that is not what the record shows. God did not leave Isaiah to wallow in his self-reproach in a "sense of sinfulness and fear." Rather, God cleansed Isaiah and then appointed him to service (see Isaiah 6:6-9). To stop at the point of self-reproach is to abort the work of God in our lives.

To carry on in this writer's line of thought tends to produce other wrong concepts also. "God punishes sin, even in those who are redeemed," the author says. It's true that God does chasten his own, as Hebrews 12:5-12 makes clear: "God disciplines us for our good, that we may share in his holiness" (v. 10). But God does not punish his own people by taking vengeance or retribution. Jesus already bore the penalty when he took on himself the punishment that we deserved for our sin.

There is a vast difference between punishing and correcting, between repaying a wrongdoer and retraining him.

I wish this were as far as the author had gone; but he went even further. He writes, "Jesus' very presence was intimidating." Several examples purport to show that Jesus terrified people. The woman who was healed by touching Jesus' garment afterward fell down before him "trembling with fear" (Mark 5:33). The writer says, "The word *trembling* is the word used in the Septuagint to describe the shaking of Mt. Sinai when God gave the law. She really shook! She was terrified. A sinner in the presence of the Holy God should be."

Pardon me?

To take this position makes Jesus a minister of Law. It ignores what Jesus said to this woman who came to him trembling. He said, "Go in peace and be freed from your suffering" (v. 34). That doesn't sound intimidating to me.

Another example cited is Peter, who at the very beginning of his association with Jesus was overwhelmed by the large catch of fish he took at Jesus' bidding. Peter said, "Go away from me, Lord; I am a sinful man!" (Luke 5:8). The writer comments "All he could see was his own sinfulness when confronted with the power and presence of Holy God. The true worshipper comes in that spirit. He is broken over his sinfulness."

But what did Jesus say to Peter in this circumstance? "Don't be afraid; from now on you will catch men" (v. 10).

To portray Jesus as Holy God who intimidates sinful

man is to risk obscuring the whole point of the gospel. Jesus came to mediate between Holy God and sinful man; to reconcile, not to intimidate.

I have no question that the writer's purpose is worthy and his concern is genuine. Like the rest of us, he wants all believers to develop a sense of reverence and awe for the Lord. And that Lord *is* holy!

But we fall into an error that is, alas, only too common. We imagine that the way to glorify God is to abase man. We think God's glory requires man's humiliation. The same writer paraphrases our Lord's "blessed are the poor in spirit" with the demeaning "blessed are the nobodies."

Is our God the God of the nobodies? Does that glorify him? Or would he receive more glory to be God of the somebodies? We read in Hebrews that when it comes to people of faith, "God is not ashamed to be called their God" (11:16). He doesn't view us as nobodies!

It's really quite the opposite. We read that God has a rich and glorious inheritance in the saints (not *for* the saints, though that's also true, but God sees us as his rich and glorious inheritance—see Ephesians 1:18). Jude tells us we are to be presented "before his glorious presence without fault and with great joy" (v. 24). We will be honored in the court of Almighty God.

We aren't nobodies. And God's glory doesn't need our self-loathing.

Whenever I encounter these how-vile-before-God-we-miserable-sinners-are teachings, my heart cries out, *Hey, haven't you heard? The war is over! God and his people have been reconciled. We aren't at loggerheads with God any more. We are not at odds. We are on the same side!*

Scripture states it even more strongly: "He who unites himself with the Lord is one with him in spirit" (1 Corinthians 6:17).

Was Jesus Wrong about the Prodigal?

To tell God's people that they always need to feel rotten about their sins is foreign to the spirit of the gospel, as portrayed in Jesus' story of the prodigal son (see Luke 15). As soon as that boy reached home, he was fully accepted and made the honored guest at a celebration.

The father didn't say, "Now, listen! I hope you realize how unworthy of forgiveness you are. You had better watch your step in the future if you expect to stay around here."

That father did not intimidate his boy; he loved him.

A sense of shame and failure may have been useful at one point if it helped bring the boy home. Perhaps his shame helped him come to his senses and choose his father's house over the miserable life in the far country. Like Betty in the previous chapter, he was at the end as well as at the bottom, and he may have gone home just to survive. In any case, the father laid no guilt trip on him once he reached home.

Suppose the son had been admitted back into the home on a "trial" basis. Suppose he had been constantly reminded of his failure. That would still have constituted better treatment than he deserved.

Knowing how bad things were in the far country, he likely would have stayed and served faithfully. But he also would have suffered emotionally from the constant reminder of his second-class status.

The elder brother would no doubt have been happy, and those who have the spirit of the elder brother are with us still.

But the father didn't see things that way. In his view, he and his son were reconciled. His son was restored as a son, not a servant.

That's grace! That's the gospel! And it shouldn't be compromised in the name of worship or holiness or anything else.

Jesus taught that those who are forgiven most will love most. And forgiven means *forgiven*. It is love and grace that keep the believer true to God, not intimidation.

Be Holy Because I Am Holy

The question is raised and must be faced: But what if a person presumes on God's love and grace? What if he carelessly or willfully sins against the light he has? Can he do absolutely anything and still be held guiltless?

Whenever a question like that arises in Scripture, words of warning follow. "As obedient children, do not conform to the evil desires you had when you lived in ignorance. But just as he who called you is holy, so be holy in all you do; for it is written: 'Be holy, because I am holy.' Since you call on a Father who judges each man's work impartially, live your lives as strangers here in reverent fear" (1 Peter 1:14-17).

Many people want firm doctrinal statements that spell out clearly just what will happen under what circumstances. They think they should have a neat system that answers all questions. But God is bigger than all our systems, and so is God's truth.

The Bible's message of grace is clear. So are its warnings against sin. We don't need to pinpoint the place where one impinges on another.

What we need to remember is that, in essence, Christianity is a relationship, not a set of rules or a list of behaviors. A person knows—*you know*—whether you have turned your face or your back toward God. To use scriptural terms: You know whether you are united to the Lord in one spirit or alienated from him.

So long as you and the Lord are on the same side, living godly will be as Betty Hunt understood it from that first day—not always easy, but always something you and your Friend can handle together.

Toward Less Moral Blindness

However genuine our love and devotion to God are, we can and do still fail him. It's so easy to think otherwise, to assume that if anything were seriously amiss in our lives the Holy Spirit would surely convict us of it. But it's not quite that simple.

Let me illustrate.

It is generally known that John Newton, who gave us one of the great hymns of all times in "Amazing Grace," was once a slave trader. What many don't know is that he continued in the slave trade long after he gave his heart and life to Christ.

He didn't realize he was sinning.

Newton had been a hard-living, profane seaman when at age twenty-two he almost perished in a storm at sea. Crying aloud to God for mercy, he was converted then and there, March 10, 1748. Immediately his life changed. His swearing ceased and he became a wonder to his fellow seamen, before whom he openly read his Bible and prayed.

Before his conversion, Newton had seen enough, one would think, to make him well aware of how wrong the slave trade was. He had worked on slave ships and witnessed the inhumane conditions firsthand. He knew the males were kept in chains down in the cargo hold, while the females were abused on deck at the whim of the crew.

Newton had also learned by experience that these blacks were human beings. During one of his early misadventures, he had been thrown into an African slave compound himself. Without food and shackled by the ankles, he would have died except that the very blacks whom he had driven with whips had compassion and took care of him.

Yet neither this nor his conversion led Newton to renounce slave trading. From 1750 to 1754, he commanded a slave ship—and held Sunday services for crew and human cargo alike. Talk about screaming inconsistency!

Almost thirty years later Newton wrote that nothing could have induced him to continue in the slave trade had he known it was wrong. "Though my religious views were not very clear, my conscience was very tender and I dared not have displeased God by acting against the light of my mind."

Newton said he never suspected his acts were wrong. To us—and even to Newton himself thirty years after the fact—that's hard to understand. To Newton's credit, he later actively supported the effort to abolish the slave trade. He played a significant role in a twenty-year struggle which ended in the abolition of slavery throughout the commonwealth in 1807, the same year that Newton died.

My question is this: How could he have blindly supported and participated in the evil of slave trading for six years after his conversion? More unsettling yet: What comparable evils may exist unsuspected in our own lives?

American Atrocities: Can It Be?

M. Scott Peck in his provocative book *People of the Lie* discusses evil from the perspective of a psychiatrist and a committed Christian. The book is awesome, and its claims and implications should be widely studied.

Most of the book focuses on individual evil. But Peck also writes about what he learned as an army psychiatrist when in 1972 he chaired a committee to recommend research on the My Lai massacre. American soldiers there murdered at least 500-600 Vietnamese men, women, and children in an atrocity that most of us have been quick to forget. Peck sees not only that atrocity but also the entire American war in Vietnam as evil. He writes:

> But how could we—we Americans—be villains? The Germans and the Japanese in 1941, certainly. The Russians, yes. But

the Americans? Surely we are not a villain-
ous people. If we were villains, we must
have been unwitting ones. This I concede;
we were largely unwitting. But how does
it come about that a person or a group or
an entire nation is an unwitting villain?
This is the crucial question.

This is a crucial question for all of us. Peck answers
the question by citing laziness and narcissism as "the twin
progenitors" of evil. Regarding the Vietnam war, he says:

As a people we were too lazy to learn and
too arrogant to think we needed to learn.
We felt that whatever way we happened to
perceive things was the right way without
any further study, and that whatever we
did was the right thing to do without re-
flection. We were so wrong because we
never seriously considered that we might
not be right. With our laziness and narcissism feeding each other, we marched off to
impose our will on the Vietnamese people
by bloodshed with practically no idea of
what was involved.[2]

Not everyone will agree with Peck about the Vietnam war being an American evil, though he makes a far
stronger case than I can report here. The point is that the
question of our culpability in Vietnam needs to be asked
and answered just as slavery needed to be questioned in
Newton's time. To refuse to ask the question betrays the
narcissism—the uncritical self-admiration—that Peck laments. To ask but not to pursue the answer betrays the
laziness he cites.

Today there are many issues which raise moral questions of which we all ought to be aware. To name a few:

world hunger
waste of food and resources

environmental pollution
domestic violence
the arms race—nuclear, germ, space
  warfare
women's rights
prison reform
racial equality
genetic engineering
religious bigotry
abortion
bureaucracy
materialism
specialization
medical care
intervention in foreign affairs
drug and alcohol abuse
tobacco price supports
state-sponsored gambling

Narcissism and laziness will lead us into unintentional evil in these and other areas. Narcissism, because in uncritical self-admiration we assume our own view must be the correct one. Laziness, because we just won't put forth the effort to study, debate, and sort out the truth.

Granted, one hasn't the time to be an expert on everything; but most of us could know a lot more than we do. We can, at least, recognize the danger of error created by our lack of understanding, and thus reduce the narcissistic arrogance that gives error its strength.

The Hope for Failing God Less

Let's summarize what we've said. We began the previous chapter with the story of Betty Hunt, a women who failed God dismally. Betty's life changed when her guilty self-hate was replaced by a sense of God's forgiveness. There is grace for those who have failed, and that grace not only forgives past failure but also gives strength to do better in the future.

Next we said that we fail God even after we become Christians, but that it doesn't invalidate our spiritual experience. Our reconciliation to God is a profound reality; we are united to him in one spirit. We are on his side now, and we must stop thinking in the old adversarial mode as if God and his people were rivals.

We said, third, that grace is not a license to sin and that God calls us to holiness. We tend to suffer from moral blindness and do wrong, as John Newton did, without even suspecting it. We attributed this blindness (at least in part) to laziness and uncritical self-admiration.

These two "progenitors of evil" are not easy to overcome, but *guess who can do it*.

Not the person who has such a load of guilt and self-loathing that he groans under its sheer weight.

Not the nobody.

Not the prodigal who has come home, but still lives in shame and under suspicion.

Not the intimidated.

Not the wretch.

Ah, but the forgiven, the strong, the hopeful, God's somebodies . . . they can endure the necessary self-criticism to see their own evil, because they operate from a secure position of union with God. They can wrestle with moral dilemma and search tirelessly for truth, for they have the energy of the Holy Spirit.

For those who know they have failed God and been forgiven, there is—at last—hope!

NOTES

1. John MacArthur Jr., *The Ultimate Priority* (Chicago: Moody Press, 1983), pp. 77-86 for this and subsequent quotes.

2. M. Scott Peck, *People of the Lie* (New York: Simon and Schuster, 1983).

4
When You Don't Feel Spiritual

Troughs and Dark Nights

Probably every Christian of two years' standing or more knows what it is to feel unspiritual. To all of us, God sometimes seems distant. We are dry, even dusty-dry, in our souls.

More than 500 years ago, Thomas à Kempis wrote a spiritual classic, *Imitation of Christ*. He confessed, "I have found no man so religious or devout that feeleth not sometime withdrawing of grace or diminution of fervor."

Another impressive example is Brother Lawrence, the simple seventeenth-century cook from whose letters were compiled *The Practice of the Presence of God*. He seemed to be in constant fellowship with the Lord. When his times of prayer were over, he "continued with God, praising and blessing Him with all his might, so that he passed his life in continual joy." Yet even he wrote of "those times of dryness or insensibility and irksomeness in prayer, by which God tries our love to Him."

When Communion Isn't

Though one might feel unspiritual at any time, the communion service frequently makes one aware of such feelings. It's supposed to be such a sacred time—and when it isn't, we can become anxious.

Several things about communion tend to make it a spiritual peak experience. First, it focuses on the suffering our Lord Jesus Christ endured for us. The elements represent his body and blood. The accompanying words remind us that he died for us personally: "This is my body given for you" (Luke 22:19).

Second, if we come to the table properly, we have examined our hearts and lives before the Lord, confessing our sins and receiving his forgiveness.

It is hard to think of any spiritual exercises better calculated to bring us into felt communion with God. Aware of our sin and of his grace, we worship him.

Still, the communion service sometimes comes up short on the communion aspect; it decays into just another service. It becomes mechanical, like all our other "acts of worship." Like those times when we feel our prayers go bouncing off the ceiling. Like when our Bible reading degenerates into a fruitless exercise that we continue only out of a dogged sense of faithfulness—that is, if we continue it at all.

The Struggle to Sense God's Presence

I remember one communion service especially well. There was no particular reason for me to feel estranged from God. The edge was simply off my spiritual sensitivity. Our communion services were becoming routine and flat. In twenty years as pastor, I had probably administered the Lord's Supper at least 300 times.

On this occasion, I decided to bring the problem to the Lord openly, before the whole congregation at the communion service. I suspected others felt as I did, and would identify with my monologue.

Lord, sometimes I feel your presence.
Sometimes I don't, not even in church.

Sometimes I really don't; I sense your absence.

Jesus, are you here?

What about that song that describes me? The song that goes, "My heart is night, my soul is steel; I cannot see, I cannot feel . . ."

Ah, yes, Lord, I know it continues,
"For light, for life, I must appeal
In simple faith to Jesus."

But am I kidding myself when I say you are here unknown to our senses? Jesus, are you really here? I mean, it is only a song.

Wait! What was that you said when you walked the earth long ago? The line we almost always hear at prayer meeting when our numbers are small: "For where two or three come together in my name, there am I with them" (Matthew 18:20).

There am I.

Then, Lord, you really are here.

We worship you, Lord, and ask you to prepare our hearts to partake of your supper.

I don't know that we produced more sense of Christ's presence that day, but we did openly and honestly confront the problem. The response of some of the members made it clear that it was a problem they shared.

The Shame of Feeling Indifferent

It *is* a problem when our most sacred times become stale. Here we are surveying the wondrous cross on which the Prince of Glory died, and we are unmoved. If we feel anything, it is shame and consternation over our own hardness of heart. Such a condition of soul is well-depicted by the nineteenth-century poet Christina Rossetti:

Am I a stone and not a sheep
That I can stand, O Christ, beneath thy
     cross
To number, drop by drop, thy blood's
     slow loss
And yet not weep?

Not so those women loved,
Who with exceeding grief lamented thee.
Not so fallen Peter, weeping bitterly.
Not so the thief was moved.

Not so the sun and moon
Which hid their faces in a starless sky,
A horror of great darkness at broad noon.
I, only I.

Yet give not o'er
But seek thy sheep, true Shepherd of the
     flock;
Greater than Moses, turn and look once
     more.
And smite a rock.

What is the true nature of our problem when we don't feel spiritual? And what can we do about it? Those questions will occupy our thoughts through this chapter and the next.

Cause One: "The Law of Undulation"
Many Causes

Spiritual doldrums such as we have been describing do not always spring from the same cause. At least three different phenomena, in addition to simple discouragement, can cast down our souls. This chapter considers two causes, and the next chapter deals with the third.

One cause of unspiritual feelings relates to what C. S. Lewis, in *The Screwtape Letters,* called "the law of undulation." Human beings, he says, experience troughs and peaks in all areas of their lives. Thus he has the demon Screwtape tell his protégé Wormwood, "The dryness and dullness through which your patient is now going are not, as you fondly suppose, your workmanship; they are merely a natural phenomenon which will do you no good unless you make a good use of it."

Our times of spiritual dullness are likely to be of this sort. Certainly God could override all of this. He could manifest his presence in ways that are always sweetness and light. He could, as it were, bridge all the troughs. Indeed, it seems that he sometimes does so for new believers. But not for the long run. If he did, there would be no opportunity for our faith and faithfulness to ripen and mature.

A Time for Faith to Shine

Faith, we read, is "being sure of what we hope for and certain of what we do not see" (Hebrews 11:1). To be certain of God when we see (or feel or sense) him is easy, but faith believes in God in the absence of any such manifestations. "This is what the ancients were commended for" (v. 2).

To God, faith is as important in us as it was in the ancients. We are not only saved through faith initially, but we are to walk by faith throughout our lives. "We live by faith, not by sight" (2 Corinthians 5:7). It is in the troughs that faith has opportunity to work.

It seems odd, but it's entirely possible that God is most pleased with us when we feel least spiritual. It is then we are walking most by faith, without which it is impossible to please him.

When you don't feel spiritual, then, seize the moment. Perhaps you cannot leap to heights of spiritual joy just now, but you can plod along the paths of God by faith.

You can be a part of that great and age-long company of faithful believers of whom we read, "Therefore God is not ashamed to be called their God" (Hebrews 11:16).

Screwtape says, "[God] wants them to learn to walk and must therefore take away His hand; and if only the will to walk is really there he is pleased even with their stumbles. Do not be deceived, Wormwood. Our cause is never more in danger than when a human, no longer desiring, but still intending to do our Enemy's will, looks round upon a universe from which every trace of Him seems to have vanished, and asks why he has been forsaken, and still obeys."

Cause Two: The Dark Night of the Soul
When Darkness Closes In

A second phenomenon can make a person feel decidedly unspiritual. It is like the first, except the trough becomes a deep, unbridged chasm that threatens to swallow one completely and forever.

Catherine Spencer came to know Christ at the age of twelve and served him all her life. In her fifties she thought her battles of faith were behind her. If there was anything she was sure of, it was the rock steadfastness of her relationship with her Lord.

And then night fell.

God disappeared.

He was still *somewhere,* she had no doubt of that, but he wasn't with her.

When reading the Scripture failed to speak to her heart, Catherine thought, *Well, I didn't get anything out of that—the wrong portion, I guess. Tomorrow I'll try John.*

But though the Gospel of John had always before nurtured her soul, this time it seemed only empty words on paper. She tried to pray, but what was once sweet communion with God had become a monologue. She felt like a person locked out of her own home, knowing she had a key but frustrated over her inability to find it.

As the almost tangible void persisted, Catherine found it devastating to her relationship with other Christians. The glow on her fellow believers, especially those new in the faith, only accented the drab emptiness she felt within.

Catherine's insensitivity toward God contrasted sharply with her sensitivity toward people, especially in the innuendo of her friends. They weren't blunt about it (of course), but somehow the message came through that "You were not so good a Christian as you thought, or you wouldn't be feeling as you do now."

Catherine didn't believe that at all. She *knew* she had walked with God. The veiled accusations made her feel more alone. She began to let the phone go unanswered.

For about six months Catherine's dark night continued. Much of the time she felt like she was hanging on by her fingernails. Then one morning Catherine knelt to pray as usual and found beauty. Her communion with God was restored. She had not shed the desolation like a garment so that it would never return. But the bad times were fewer and less severe, and she knew she could manage.

In Catherine's case the dawn came slowly—but it did come, and today she is fully restored. The ordeal was still fresh in her mind when I talked with her last, and tears blurred her eyes as she described it. She had come far enough through, however, to analyze what had happened. She perceived four stages.

1. *Desperation.* She had lost contact with God, and no amount of praying, reading Scripture, or listening to Christian teaching helped in the slightest.

2. *Defiance.* She decided that if she had to walk by faith without any sense of communion with God, she would do that. "Who needs it?" she told herself. "I'll just keep on keeping on."

3. *Desolation*. She plunged into a black hole. She was like a child needing to hold on to her father's hand—but she was all alone. Already it seemed she had spent an eternity in this living hell, and for all she knew it might continue as long as she lived.

4. *Hope*. She began to see tiny glimpses of light, small as pinpricks. One day while walking down the aisle of a hospital, she overheard a snatch of conversation from a stranger. What the woman was talking about, Catherine never knew, but the words "It's true," pierced her heart. "Oh, Lord," she cried from the depths of her being, "I know it's true. I don't know what happened to it, but I know it's true."

Shortly after that episode, her communion with God was reborn. Dark times still creep in, "but those times are shorter now and not so deep," she said, a smile glistening through her tears.

I knew she would be all right.

Why Does the Dark Night Come?

I suspect that inexplicable dark nights of the soul like Catherine's are uncommon. They are far from unknown, however, and should not be dismissed lightly.

The expression "dark night of the soul" originated, as far as anyone can tell, with the sixteenth-century Spanish mystic named St. John of the Cross (who wrote a book by that title). The phrase was later borrowed by Georgia Harkness for her own book, published in 1945. Her book describes dark-night experiences of believers of all ages, including George Fox, John Bunyan, and Madame Guyon.

Harkness linked the dark night to depression, perfectionism, and other emotional ills. She suggested it involves both sin and illness, even though it usually afflicts "better" Christians. She did not think it sent arbitrarily by

God to refine the soul, though he certainly might use it to that end.

In contrast to Harkness, St. John of the Cross insisted that the dark night was to be distinguished from distress caused by sin or emotional disorders. He held that to imply that those in the dark night are suffering from "melancholy or some other imperfection with respect to sense or to spirit" is to play Job's comforters and accuse the innocent.

Maybe it can work either way. Maybe the dark night can result from emotional and spiritual problems or can come without regard to either.

Is It Depression by Another Name?

Don Baker in his book *Depression* describes his own feelings of separation from God in terms that sound like a dark-night experience.

> For hours each day I would ponder such questions as:
>
> Where is God?
>
> Why doesn't he answer me?
>
> Has God really deserted me?
>
> My theology rejected the last possibility, but my life seemingly had nothing to show for his abiding presence.
>
> My Bible kept saying to me that God is a changeless God, and yet it seemed that without explanation he suddenly had become terribly indifferent.
>
> This God of mine, who had promised never to leave or forsake, appeared now to be playing some cruel form of hide and seek. No matter how diligently I sought him, he was nowhere to be found.
>
> This God whom I had loved and served

had promised to keep his ears open to my cries. When I prayed, however, it seemed that he had now become stone deaf.

My Bible, always a source of strength, had little to say to me. When it did speak, the words were soon lost in the pall of gloom and forgetfulness that had settled down over my mind.

Time and again I would leaf through its pages, seeking a promise or an explanation, only to close its covers in disappointment.[1]

Baker at length discovered that he was hypoglycemic, and he attributed some of his difficulties to that. He also writes of demonic influence and of being ambitious beyond his abilities, suggesting a complex mix of factors for his depression.

By contrast, Catherine Spencer (and St. John of the Cross) seemed to experience the dark night apart from any discernible cause. Individual cases apparently can arise from wholly different causes.

What Does the Bible Say?

The Scriptures never talk about a dark night of the soul by that term. No character in Scripture serves as a clear example of such, though Job, Jeremiah, and even David are possible cases.

But one unique psalm, the eighty-eighth, does paint a picture of the soul's dark night. Alexander MacLaren says it "stands alone in the psalter, which would be incomplete as a mirror of phases of devout experience unless it had one psalm expressing trust which has ceased to ask or hope . . . but still clasps God's hand even in the 'darkness.'"

The unique thing about the psalm is not that the

writer feels deep anguish. It is not that God fails to answer his prayer. It is that he cannot get through to God at all. "But I cry to you for help, O LORD; in the morning my prayer comes before you. Why, O LORD, do you reject me and hide your face from me?" (vv. 13-14). The psalm ends in unrelieved despair. "The darkness is my closest friend."

Let There Be Light

So, then . . . what else is there to say? Our attempt to understand the dark night of the soul remains ill-defined, like the experience itself. But that does not mean there is nothing to be done, or that there is no hope. Far from it.

The first thing to do is to repent of all known sin. Certainly it is cruel and unfair for someone else to say or imply that your problem is unconfessed sin; but you do need to face that possibility. Sin *does* separate people from God. "Surely the arm of the LORD is not too short to save, nor his ear too dull to hear. But your iniquities have separated you from your God; your sins have hidden his face from you, so that he will not hear" (Isaiah 59:1-2).

A second thing to do is to get a thorough physical checkup. Don't settle for a cursory examination. Tell your doctor about the depression or darkness you are experiencing. Ask him to eliminate all possible physical causes. Don't be afraid to specify that you want a blood sugar test for hypoglycemia, and adrenal and thyroid tests. These days it is appropriate for patients to "take an interest" in their own case. If your doctor resents it or is uncooperative, perhaps you should see a different doctor.

In addition to the above-mentioned tests, if you are a young adult, you should be checked for mononucleosis. If you are a woman in menopause, you should be checked for hormonal imbalance.

A third place to seek remedy for spiritual darkness is counseling. If your own pastor or church counselor doesn't suit you, inquire about other resources in your area. Call local mental health agencies, check the yellow pages, ask recommendations of your friends. Larger cities and many mid-sized ones have Christian counseling centers, some of which base their rates on ability to pay.

Fourth, take good care of yourself. Get plenty of rest and exercise. Eat properly and use vitamins judiciously. Keep busy with constructive activities, giving yourself something else to think about besides your condition.

Fifth, keep hanging on to God. Trust his sovereignty and his love. Remember that you are indwelt by Jesus Christ. I know this will seem hard to do. "Where is God?" you may still ask. "Why this darkness? Will there ever be light again?"

Come back with me to the opening words of the Bible. "In the beginning God created the heavens and the earth. Now the earth was formless and empty, darkness was over the surface of the deep" (Genesis 1:1-2). Does that also sound like a description of your soul?

Then read on. "And the Spirit of God was hovering over the waters. And God said, 'Let there be light,' and there was light" (vv. 2-3).

I say it again. Keep hanging on to God. He raises the dead and calls into being that which was not. He once brooded over a whole world shrouded in darkness and then declared, "Let there be light," and there was light.

Your day, too, will dawn.

NOTES

1. Don Baker, *Depression: Finding Hope and Meaning in Life's Darkest Shadow* (Portland, Oregon: Multnomah Press, 1983), pp. 65, 66.

5
When Comfort Is Worse Than Pain

The Problem of Painlessness

Much has been written in recent times about *The Problem of Pain*, as C. S. Lewis called his book on suffering. *Where Is God When It Hurts?* is Philip Yancey's book on the same subject.

These are good books and they address a difficult theological and personal question: Why does a God of love permit suffering?

When we ask ourselves why we sometimes don't feel spiritual, we are confronting an issue intrinsically related to suffering.

A basic concept we need to grasp is this: *As bad as pain can be, painlessness is worse.*

This is true in a cosmic sense—God chose to make man even though he knew man would fall. Our Lord chose to experience the pain of man's fall and redemption over the painlessness of a universe without man.

True to his Father's principles, Jesus chose the pain of the incarnation and the cross over the painlessness of staying in glory and forgetting about humanity.

We sometimes make an opposite choice. We take the painless way. We choose the comfortable over the challenging, the easy over the meaningful, the safe over the rewarding. And each time we make a wrong choice of this kind, we forfeit a chunk of life.

After a few crucial bad decisions or a long list of smaller ones, we begin to wonder where our vitality went. Why are our prayers listless, our devotions routine, our entire lives boring? "Where is God when it hurts" is not our anguished question at those times. We've successfully dodged life's hurts. Our heart-cry—somewhere deep down under layers of indifference—is, "Where is God when it *doesn't* hurt?"

Who Needs Pain?

We have said that choosing painlessness leads to spiritual boredom. Does that mean we should seek to suffer in order to be fully alive to God? No. But neither should the desire to avoid pain deter us from doing the will of God when it involves suffering . . . *as it will*.

Some are vocal in teaching a contrary concept. Jesus said he came that we might have life abundantly (see John 10:10). Some interpret "abundant" to mean "painless." We should be prospering materially, physically, and spiritually, they say, not hurting in any of these areas.

Scripture Misused

One passage used to support this view is 3 John 2: "Beloved, I wish above all things that thou mayest prosper and be in health, even as thy soul prospereth" (KJV).

Please don't be offended if you have understood this to be God's message to you; but let me remind you of the important principles of Bible interpretation we stated previously (chapter 1). Not every statement in the Bible is a direct or even an indirect promise to us personally. We need to ask at least two questions about a passage in question:

1. Is this a message from God to Christians generally?

2. Does the suggested interpretation square with the rest of the Bible?

First, our passage from 3 John 2 is clearly a personal message from one friend to another—"the elder, to my dear friend Gaius" (v. 1). It is essentially a warm greeting and an expression of good will. The *New International Version* renders it, "Dear friend, I pray that you may enjoy good health and that all may go well with you, even as your soul is getting along well."

At the end of this brief letter, John writes, "I hope to see you soon, and we will talk face to face" (v. 14). Should we use that verse to teach that people should expect God will soon appear to them personally? Should they claim that "promise" and try by faith to make it a reality?

Hardly. Neither the opening greeting nor the farewell constitutes a promise from God to his people.

Second, although one could argue that the Bible envisions believers becoming prosperous in every area of life (with passages such as Joshua 1:8, Psalm 1, and John 10:10), there are other passages which must modify that concept.

"In this world you will have trouble," Jesus promised (John 16:33). "Has not God chosen those who are poor in the eyes of the world to be rich in faith?" asks James (James 2:5). "I know your afflictions and your poverty— yet you are rich! . . . Do not be afraid of what you are about to suffer," the Lord told the church at Smyrna (Revelation 2:9-10).

Prosperity teachings may be fine up to a point; but they are both false and damaging when pressed so far that they imply a good Christian should enjoy a life without pain.

No Struggle, No Strength

The church at Laodicea was characterized by people who said, "I am rich; I have acquired wealth and do not need a thing" (Revelation 3:17). Not coincidentally, God said they were "neither cold nor hot. I wish you were either one or the other! So, because you are lukewarm— neither hot nor cold—I am about to spit you out of my mouth" (vv. 15-16).

They had no pain. They were also spiritually blasé.

Dr. C.I. Scofield said years ago in another context, "Of all the needy classes of people, the neediest of this earth are not those who are having a heartbreaking, agonizing struggle for victory, but those who are having no struggle at all, and no victory, and who do not know it, and who are satisfied and jogging along in a pitiable ab- sence of almost all the possessions that belong to them in Christ."

Note it—one can be satisfied spiritually and yet be pitiable. God has something better in mind for us than a painless, empty Nirvana. He wants us to know the incred- ible excitement of sharing in the life of God as his friend.

Friendship with God Means Sharing His Suffering

To say you don't feel spiritual can be another way of saying that your friendship with the Lord is not what it once was. You and he have taken divergent paths.

It's hard to maintain any friendship when paths di- verge. My best friend in high school (and afterward) was Bill Smith. We spent many hours together and confided in one another. I was best man at his wedding and he was best man at mine.

Then I went into Bible college and Bill went into business. I began to think he wasn't very spiritual, and I suppose he began to think I was a fanatic. Perhaps there was some truth to both.

In any case, our personal interests diverged and our friendship cooled. We located in different cities and lost touch. Years later, residing near each other and of like mind again, we renewed our friendship. Today it's a source of satisfaction to both of us.

Friendship with God doesn't depend on geography, since he dwells everywhere. But it does depend on mutual interest and concerns. Bob Pierce, founder of World Vision, caught the spirit of friendship with God when he said, "Let my heart be broken with the things that break the heart of God." If you don't care about God's concerns, you should not be surprised that you feel unspiritual.

The Man Called God's Friend

One man in history was especially known as the friend of God. "'Abraham believed God, and it was credited to him as righteousness' and he was called God's friend" (James 2:23, see also 2 Chronicles 20:7 and Isaiah 41:8).

Being God's friend did not mean Abraham would spend his life being lulled to sleep by soft music and gentle breezes. It meant he shared God's willingness to endure pain for a purpose.

Abraham began his friendship with God by leaving his home and kindred for a promised inheritance that was miles away and years distant. He gave up the comforts of the city to spend his life in tents. He later experienced the pain of wanting but not having a son, then of sending away a son born of Hagar, then of offering up the long-awaited son of promise on Mt. Moriah . . . and much more.

Suppose that after Abraham came to know God, he had decided deep inside that he didn't want all this pain. Suppose he had settled permanently in Haran or had moved back to Ur. Would he have become known as the friend of God? I doubt it. And I doubt he would have felt spiritual, even if he had led an exemplary life as a man of God in Ur. He'd have known the problem of painlessness, the lack of an exciting presence of God in his life. He and God would have been of divergent minds, and not friends.

So if you wonder where God is, don't think the question of spirituality is settled by how you rate on some chart of dos and don'ts. The question is, have you obeyed God's call to a life of faith and purpose, even though that involves pain?

Being a Friend of Jesus

Jesus once said to His disciples, "I no longer call you servants, because a servant does not know his master's business. Instead, I have called you friends, for everything that I learned from my Father I have made known to you" (John 15:15).

One basic thing Jesus learned from his Father was this principle of *no gain without pain*. He taught his disciples about it this way: "Unless a kernel of wheat falls to the ground and dies, it remains only a single seed. But if it dies, it produces many seeds" (John 12:24).

Immediately after calling them friends, Jesus told his disciples that "You did not choose me, but I chose you to go and bear fruit—fruit that will last" (John 15:16). God's priority for us is that we be fruitful, not comfortable. When we choose to the contrary, we diverge from God's plan, our friendship with the Lord suffers, and we don't feel spiritual because we aren't.

The Pain We Don't Need

There are, of course, distortions of the principle we've been describing. One distortion is to establish a sort of misery test for Christianity. The notion is that if dodging pain leads to an unspiritual life, then the more we suffer the more spiritual we must be. The next step beyond that is to let our suffering be known so people will realize how spiritual we are.

Jesus said the hypocrites of his day looked somber and "they disfigure their faces to show men they are fasting" (Matthew 6:16). In our day we sometimes encounter sad-faced "Christians" who display their pain like a badge of righteousness and who look like they were baptized in pickle juice.

One thing the Christian community doesn't need more of is this pain-loving martyr type. When even a few of us take that route, it is too many. We not only experience pain, but we are a pain. Self-righteous people are always obnoxious to God and man alike.

Another distortion is represented by the pain-seeking emotional disorder called *masochism,* which is defined broadly as "any pleasure obtained from being abused or dominated." This also is definitely not pain of a godly sort.

To distinguish constructive pain from the destructive is not difficult. The pain we are called upon to suffer for God is always incidental. It is never our focus and never an end in itself. We don't seek it. All we seek is to live productive and faithful lives. The pain is simply there.

Must We Suffer Forever?

Though painlessness may be linked to spiritual dullness in this life, it does not follow that we must suffer forever in order to be fully alive forever.

Scripture describes the New Jerusalem like this: "Now the dwelling of God is with men, and he will live with them. They will be his people, and God himself will be with them and be their God. He will wipe every tear from their eyes. There will be no more death or mourning or crying or pain, for the old order of things has passed away" (Revelation 21:3-4).

Notice that "the old order" is to disappear. What the

new order will be, we perceive only dimly. But it will not, we are told, include pain. Of course, even this statement strongly implies that pain is a normative element of the present order.

The situation seems to be this: Being a friend of God includes accepting pain now, as he does. In the new order, there will be no pain at all. Rather, "God himself will be with them and be their God." It is God's presence that makes life vital. In this life that involves pain, but hereafter it will not.

Increasing Our Tolerance for Pain

When we speak of the problem of painlessness, we aren't saying that you ought to plan on a life of agony. Pain doesn't have to be that bad.

How much will it hurt? Sometimes more and sometimes less, but always it will be abundantly worthwhile. "Even if you should suffer for what is right, you are blessed," said Peter (1 Peter 3:14). "I consider that our present sufferings are not worth comparing with the glory that will be revealed in us," said Paul (Romans 8:18).

You can also increase your tolerance for pain. When I was a boy, I was scared to death of needles. The announcement of an inoculation program at school filled me with dread. And when the shot came, the pain seemed just as bad as I had feared it would be.

At age twenty-four I came down with acute hepatitis and spent twelve days in a hospital getting acquainted with needles. There were needles for blood tests, needles for shots, needles for intravenous feeding. I soon learned to take them in stride. They still caused me pain, and sometimes sharp pain, but they were necessary to make me better.

If I have to endure some pain to do the will of God, I should be able to accept that also, knowing that God knows what he is doing and intends to make me better.

What Kind of Pain?

In fully doing the will of God, we encounter pain as understood in its broadest sense, not just physical discomfort. Have you ever heard of a skilled craftsman or artist taking pains to do a good job? That is one kind of pain that should mark our lives as children of God.

Another type of pain we need to accept is that of exercising the discipline required to live to God's glory. It sometimes hurts to make ourselves do what we should instead of what we want. It especially hurts when self-pity gets in and we start thinking how hard it is.

A remedy for self-pity is to think of what Christ bore on the cross for us. Our little pains of self-discipline don't seem like much by comparison. We can remember, too, that the Christ of the cross indwells us, and he hasn't changed. He is still willing to endure the cross for the joy to follow. We are not going to feel very spiritual if we silence the spirit of Christ in our hearts in order to choose comfort.

The Pain of Shyness

Yet a third type of pain involves relating to people for Jesus' sake. Have you ever heard of a person being painfully shy? In following God fully, such a person will endure the pain required to mix with other people.

Harry Bose immediately comes to mind as a classic example of someone painfully shy. He could hardly speak to another person in a social situation. His face turned red, he shifted his weight from one foot to the other, and when he finally spoke his voice came from way down in his throat so that you could hardly hear him.

Harry was a big, strong farmer, about thirty-five years old when I first met him. He was a bachelor, of course, since he couldn't talk to a man, much less a woman.

Harry's friend, Lloyd Porter, was just the opposite—an outgoing, fun-loving guy who seemed comfortable with everybody. Lloyd was a Christian.

It wasn't easy for Harry to accept Lloyd's invitation to come to church, involving as it did painful social contact with others. At last he came, though, and he kept on coming. Harry never did get over his shyness completely, but he did walk the aisle to receive Christ. Later he walked the aisle again when he married Sallie Hooper, whom he'd invited to church. In due time he became an elder.

In church board meetings Harry found it painful to speak up, but when he did, people listened, for he spoke with wisdom and grace. Today, more than one person has reason to be thankful that Harry did not choose the painless path.

If you follow the search for painlessness very far, you will likely end up not only out of touch with God, but out of touch with life. All will seem such a weariness.

Live, Don't Exist

Scripture says, "The widow who lives for pleasure is dead even while she lives" (1 Timothy 5:6). The principle applies equally to those who aren't widows.

Some time ago I read about a woman who seems to represent the very antithesis of being dead while she lives. *Virtue* magazine carried an interview with Ann Kiemel Anderson, who wrote a book a few years ago entitled *I'm Out to Change My World* and another called *I Love the Word Impossible*. You get the idea just from the titles that she is not a passive, bored-with-life person.

The interviewer asked Ann how she had kept her faith growing and alive over many years. She replied: "I think most people lose their enthusiasm because they lose touch with life. They don't get close to people and love them, feel with them, cry with them and hurt with them.

When you're really close to them and loving them and reaching out to them, somehow it makes Jesus so real because he's so much a part of all of that."

Not everyone is comfortable with that formulation. "I don't reach out to people in order to get close to Jesus," some say. "Rather, it's being close to Jesus that enables me to reach out to people."

If that's what is happening in your life, great. If you feel close to Jesus and as a result you are loving and serving others, you don't need any advice from me.

But I am writing to you who don't feel spiritual, and particularly to you whose doldrums trace to a Dead Sea syndrome. You have taken in and taken in, but haven't given out because of the cost, the risk, the pain.

Get close to people, love them, cry with them and hurt with them. Not only will you find Jesus is "part of all that," but you'll likely find he's freshly alive in you.

Part 2

*Getting Through
the Toughest Times*

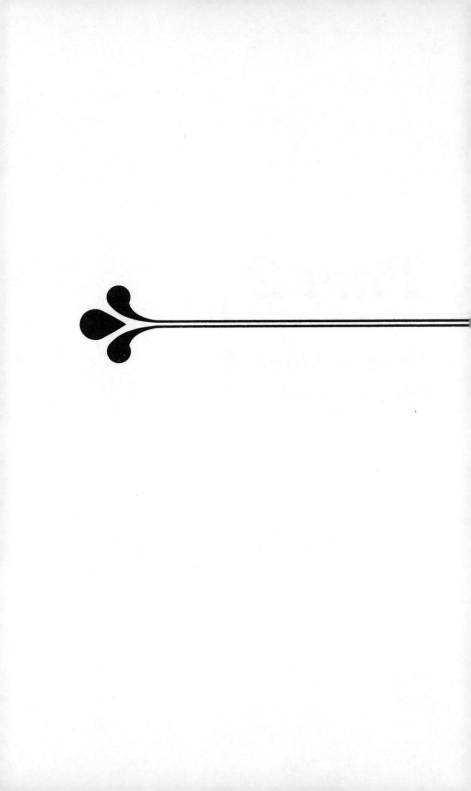

6
When You Have Every Reason to Worry

Why "Don't Worry" Is Bad Advice

WORRY: mental distress or agitation resulting from concern usually for something impending or anticipated: ANXIETY (Webster's Seventh New Collegiate Dictionary).

If you are worried about anything, you had better not show it. At least not around some of the brethren. You are likely to be whacked with a Bible passage: "Do not be anxious about anything, but in everything, by prayer and petition, with thanksgiving, present your requests to God. And the peace of God, which transcends all understanding, will guard your hearts and your minds in Christ Jesus" (Philippians 4:6-7).

"See," you are told, "the Bible says we are not to be anxious. When we are anxious, we are not trusting God. Worry is just plain sin."

Great. You have as much as ever to worry about, but now you also have a load of guilt to carry. You've just been diagnosed as living in sin.

Superficial Solutions

Most of us are adept at handling worry as long as it concerns other people's problems. Too often, like the false prophets of Jeremiah's day, we "heal the brokenness of the daughter of My people superficially, saying, 'Peace, peace,' but there is no peace" (Jeremiah 8:11 NASB).

We glibly say, "Don't worry, everything is going to be all right." Those easy words have offered but slight comfort to countless people who soon found everything was *not* going to be all right. They had every reason to worry.

A child is missing. Despite the fact that thousands of children disappear each year, never to be seen again, someone is almost certain to tell the anxious parents, "Don't worry; I'm sure you'll find her (or him) soon."

A teenager gets into trouble with the authorities. "Don't worry," a well-meaning friend tells the parents. "He (or she) will be all right. It seems they all have to sow a few wild oats." He fails to mention that some of these wild-oat sowers are only beginning a long and tragic series of wrong choices leading to misery.

A man loses his job. "Don't worry," people say. "You will find something else soon." This despite the fact that the man may be virtually unemployable because of his age and a changing job market.

Someone is sick and it's not just the flu. Doctors don't seem to know for sure what's wrong, but friends and family say, "Don't worry; you'll be all right." They say this even though some disease will sooner or later take the life of every person on earth who is not either killed or raptured.

Now, it's fine to comfort and encourage people, and I am not suggesting we predict the worst when worrisome circumstances arise: "You may never see that child again!"

No, no. But what we ought to do is speak the truth: "God cares, and God will see you through this ordeal."

What we ought not do is advocate an unworry based on a denial of reality. Sometimes people have every reason to worry, and to pretend they do not is to take residence in fantasyland.

"But if you are a Christian all things work together for good," someone says, "and everything will be all right, even if seemingly bad things happen. God's word tells us not to worry."

Still, doesn't it seem just a bit glib to dismiss worry casually? Our examples imply that the reason one shouldn't worry is that the thing feared won't happen. The fact is that the things people fear may indeed come upon them. Some certainly will.

To Worry or Not to Worry

The "mental distress for something anticipated" which the dictionary calls *worry* is actually a form of fear. Once we grasp this, we can begin to see that there is both appropriate and inappropriate worry (fear).

Some deny this. They are as critical of fear as they are of worry, and again they cite Scripture: "There is no fear in love; but perfect love casteth out fear; because fear hath torment. He that feareth is not made perfect in love" (1 John 4:18, KJV).

But we should remember what C. S. Lewis said:

> Perfect love, we know, casteth out fear. But so do several other things—ignorance, alcohol, passion, presumption, and stupidity. It is very desirable that we should all advance to that perfection of love in which we shall fear no longer, but it is very undesirable, until we have reached that stage, that we should allow any inferior agent to cast out our fear"[1]

Even in this state of imperfect love, however, fear makes no sense when:

- the anticipated event is unlikely to happen
- the consequences, even if the event happens, are relatively trivial

Worry is irrational when it causes people to fret over circumstances that fall into either of these two categories. The worrier stews and fusses because this or that *might* happen—even though the chances are perhaps 1,000 to 1 against it, or it wouldn't make that much difference anyway. He or she is agitated—and probably agitates everyone else around—because it *could* happen.

Anne has a son in eighth grade at a Christian school. To get there he has to take public transportation. Anne is worried. What if her son is delayed for some reason after school and misses the bus?

Let's test Anne's worry by the standards we've suggested. First, is the anticipated event likely to happen? Anne thinks that sooner or later it is.

Second, are the consequences of missing the bus serious or trivial? Since the city buses run every twenty minutes or so all day long and far into the night, it is a trivial matter if an eighth grader misses his bus. Anne's worry is inappropriate in light of these facts.

A Time to Worry

L. E. Maxwell, the late principal of Prairie Bible Institute, once editorially "lamented and exposed the departure of a young minister from the orthodox faith." In reaction the minister threatened to sue him for libel. Maxwell describes his worry:

> I cannot tell all the misery through which I passed during the ensuing months. I would wake up in the wee hours of the morning with my mind racing like a windmill out of control. When I would try to find a sermon to preach, my mind would

be tortured with anxiety. Even while on my knees seeking God for a message, I would be torn with fear and worry about the future. I could see myself in prison with my hair shaved off and wearing striped clothes. Even when I walked downtown I fancied I saw an officer coming to arrest me.[2]

Again, let's test the worry by the standards we've established. Was the anticipated event likely to happen? Apparently Mr. Maxwell did have reason to think he was in danger of being sued for libel.

Would the consequences be serious or trivial? Exactly how serious the consequences would be is difficult to evaluate from a distance. The best guess is that the threat was not nearly so great as Mr. Maxwell imagined.

Libel suits are hard to win. The plaintiff must show first that the statements were false, second that they were made with malice or serious negligence, third that they were actually damaging. Even then the defendant would face a financial judgment rather than a prison sentence.

Nevertheless, the consequences would have been serious. Losing a libel suit would be costly in terms of money and reputation. It would dishonor the Lord and hurt the work to which Mr. Maxwell had dedicated his life. Even if he won the suit, the charges alone could do great damage.

By our tests, then, Mr. Maxwell did have reason to worry; fear about an anticipated event was legitimate.

Although he was thoroughly familiar with the biblical admonitions against worry, and although he tried to obey them, Mr. Maxwell was unable to find peace. Ultimately he stopped worrying only when he was "quite sure the case would never come up."

Five years later in an unrelated incident, Maxwell said something on a radio broadcast that a friend commented afterward was "too much." Immediately Maxwell recalled his old libel worries: "There was no mistake about it. I recognized the same issue, the same worry, the same distraction of mind. I also sensed the finger of God's just accusation."

Note the double whammy: Worry, complicated by guilt over the failure to trust God and to obey his Word that says, "Be anxious for nothing."

At last Mr. Maxwell recognized and confessed "my unwillingness to be identified with the Cross, my secret dislike to bear shame for his name, my inward refusal to rejoice in being counted worthy to suffer reproach . . . then I knew peace."

According to this testimony, then, worry was a *friend* to grace. It brought Maxwell to embrace the cross and to a spiritual growth that would not have occurred had he been able simply to dismiss all his concern and anxiety.

Had there been nothing to fear—or had he denied the threat was real—he would not have been "crowded to Christ" in repentance and renewed faith.

Sometimes It Helps to Worry

Those who say "don't worry" commonly offer plausible arguments against it. "So God can use worry to turn people to him. He can use sin and guilt that way too, but that doesn't make them desirable or right."

"Granted, bad things sometimes do happen. It certainly doesn't help to worry about them beforehand."

"Misfortunes come whether we worry about them or not. All we do when we worry is prolong the suffering. We add worry time to our hurting time."

In some cases these statements are true. The Bible certainly does not advocate a life style dominated by worry, fear, and negative thinking. Neither should we. Case studies show, however, that appropriate worry helps in the very situations in which denial is neither beneficial nor honest.

Carl was a strong man in his early forties. He had worked outdoors all his life and his body was lean and hard. He didn't drink, he didn't smoke, and he didn't worry. He was not a high risk for heart disease, but he had it nevertheless. Doctors scheduled him for heart bypass surgery.

Carl was not worried about the surgery. The doctors assured him that such an operation was, in Carl's words, "no big deal any more"—routine, really. And his overall physical condition was very much in his favor.

I visited Carl in his hospital room the night before his surgery. He was so chipper you'd have thought he was going on vacation the next day. I didn't sense it was all a brave front, either. Carl wasn't worried.

The surgery went as routinely as the doctors had predicted, and Carl's prognosis afterward was good. A couple of days later I talked with his wife. Carl wasn't doing well. He was depressed, resentful, and angry. He was in pain. And he seemed worried—about his health, about his ability ever to do his job again, about his family, about finances. Carl eventually recovered, but his convalescence was slower and more difficult than anyone had expected. I couldn't understand it.

How You React Makes a Difference

Some time later while doing research for my book *How to Build Your Christian Character,* I ran across a report that threw considerable light on the mystery of Carl's poor recovery.

In *The Quest for Self-Control,* Dr. Irving L. Janis, Yale professor of psychology, described studies of three types of patient attitudes before surgery. Patients in the first grouping were "constantly worried and agitated." Those in the second grouping were "occasionally tense or agitated." The third grouping consisted of those who were "constantly cheerful and optimistic . . . no observable agitation or tension."

The studies concluded that:

>   1. Persons who were *extremely fearful* before the operation were *more* likely than others to be anxiety-ridden again afterwards, and their excessive fears of body damage were linked with numerous clinical signs of chronic neurotic disturbance.

>   2. Persons who displayed a *moderate* degree of preoperative fear were significantly *less* likely than others to display any form of emotional disturbance during the stressful period of postoperative convalescence.

>   3. Persons who showed a relative *absence* of preoperative fear were *more* likely than others to display disturbed reactions of anger and intense resentment during postoperative convalescence.[3]

Carl seemed to fit very well into Dr. Janis's third category. He hadn't worried about his surgery in advance and he had paid for it afterward.

In contrast to Carl, Marge was informed by her doctor before major surgery that she would have considerable pain afterward. "The third day is usually the worst," he said.

When Marge felt rotten on the third day after surgery, she remembered the doctor's words and took courage. Though she was feeling worse, it didn't mean things were going wrong. She had no reason to panic or worry. *No doubt I will feel better tomorrow,* she thought. And she did.

According to Dr. Janis, not only surgery but any

"stressful life situation" calls for "reality-oriented" worrying. Besides surgery patients, he reported on women in labor, cancer patients, civilian air-raid victims, women whose sons and husbands were sent to war, and combat pilots. In all these situations, those who worried realistically coped with stress better than those who did not.

It was also true that those who worried excessively did worst of all in coping with difficulty when it came.

Dr. Janis writes that people reveal a "powerful, spontaneous tendency to *deny* the possibility of being personally afected by an impending source of danger." In other words, some people don't worry when they should. Let me cite the ultimate example.

When Not Worrying Brings Death

An evangelist preaches the gospel. He faithfully proclaims that Christ died for our sins, was buried, and rose again. He concludes by inviting people to receive Christ as savior, and says, "Whoever believes in the Son has eternal life, but whoever rejects the Son will not see life, for God's wrath remains on him" (John 3:36).

A man hears the message and weighs his decision. The Bible says that if he rejects Christ, God's wrath will remain on him. He thinks of the absolute horror that suggests. Just at this point an inner voice says, "Don't worry, you'll be all right."

There it is—the "powerful, spontaneous tendency to deny" the danger.

My question is this: Should the man worry?

Clearly, he should. And he should continue to worry until, by turning in faith to Jesus Christ, he deals with the danger that hangs over his head.

It sometimes *does* help to worry, and never more so than when one worries enough about his relationship to God to cry out for mercy and forgiveness.

NOTES

1. C. S. Lewis, *The World's Last Night* (New York: Harcourt, Brace & Co., copyright 1952 by C. S. Lewis), p. 109.

2. L. E. Maxwell, "Worry," *Prairie Harvester,* Spring 1983.

3. Irving L. Janis, "Psychodynamic Aspects of Stress Tolerance," in *The Quest for Self Control,* ed. Samuel Z. Klausner (New York: The Free Press, a division of the Macmillan Co., 1965), p. 226.

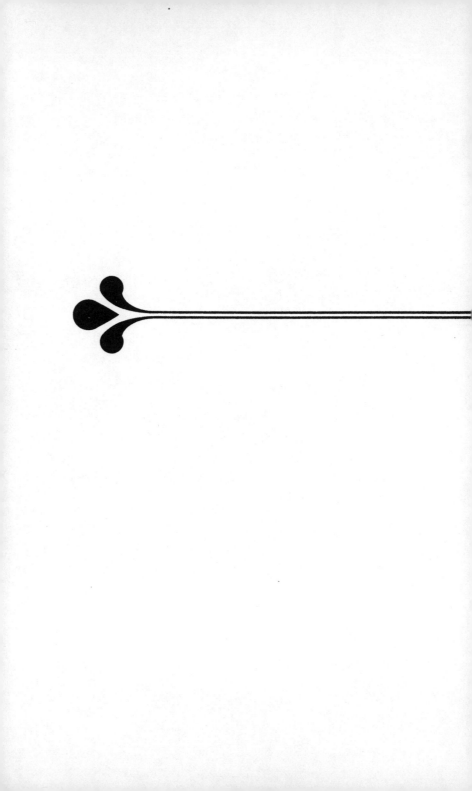

7
When Anxiety Threatens to Overwhelm You

Solving the Worry Problem

Charles Darwin knew the frustration of a worry he could not control. "I cannot enjoy the present happiness," he said, "for anticipating the future, which is about as foolish as the dog who dropped the real bone for its shadow." Even though he saw clearly the folly of his worry, he kept on worrying.

So did L. E. Maxwell, despite his knowledge of the Bible's admonitions against it.

If neither Darwin's common sense nor Maxwell's Bible knowledge solved their worry problems, what can? "The unfolding of Thy words gives light; it gives understanding to the simple" (Psalm 119:130, NASB). We need to look deeper, to really "unfold" God's word on worry.

The Worries of Paul

It is interesting that Paul, who tells us not to worry (Philippians 4:6), also seems to say in other places that he himself does worry. What can this mean?

First, it is true that concern and worry are two different things—they need to be distinguished. The dictionary says that worry is "mental distress or agitation resulting from concern . . ."

Anxiety or worry is stronger than concern. One might say that when concern takes control, it becomes worry.

In the Greek New Testament, as in English, we find two different words to describe greater and lesser degrees of care or concern. When Paul writes to "be *anxious* for nothing," he uses *merimnao*. By contrast, when he writes just a few lines further on that the Philippians have kindly renewed their *concern* for him, he uses the other word, *phroneo* (v. 10).

It all seems to work out rather neatly; we can say to go ahead and be concerned *(phroneo),* but don't let your concern become anxiety *(merimnao)*.

Unfortunately, this neat packaging comes untied when Paul uses *merimnao* to describe Timothy's commendable anxiety over the church. "I have no man likeminded, who will naturally *care* for your state." So reads Philippians 2:20 in the King James Version. The New International Version translates it with the extremely weak phrase, "takes a genuine interest." In the original it is the strong word *merimnao*.

It's worth noting that Paul describes Timothy as being likeminded with himself in this regard. Does that mean Paul worried over the Philippian church? Not only does it sound that way here, but Paul declares as much elsewhere. "Besides everything else, I face daily the pressure of my concern *(merimna)* for all the churches" (2 Corinthians 11:28).

A Prescription, Not a Condemnation

What shall we think of this seeming contradiction in Paul? He tells the Philippians not to worry but declares that he himself does.

Various explanations have been suggested. Some say it's simply a contrast between the ideal and the real. The ideal is to have no anxiety, and we should strive for that. Nevertheless, Paul was human and he admitted that he sometimes worried.

But Paul clearly laments that the only ones who worried about the churches were himself and Timothy— hardly a proper attitude to have if his worry was a weakness (or a *sin,* as some have declared it to be).

Others seek an explanation in the differing subjects of concern. In the natural, we worry about things we perceive as threats to ourselves. Worry is self-centered. That is what Paul condemned, telling the Philippians to commit their personal concerns to God in prayer instead of worrying over them. (I'm not sure how that helps, though. Wouldn't that make our *prayers* self-centered? Is that any better?)

By contrast, Paul worried about the churches, about the spiritual welfare of others rather than his own needs.

The problem with this explanation is that Paul wrote, "Be anxious for *nothing.*" He didn't distinguish between selfish and unselfish concerns. Besides, many of the worries that most torment people today are for others: for children, for mates, for friends.

Furthermore, when we worry about others we are worrying for ourselves at the same time. We love these others for whom we are concerned, and when they hurt we hurt. That is certainly how it was with Paul and the churches (see 2 Corinthians 11:29). The distinction between selfish and unselfish worry seems dubious.

A third and better explanation is that the admonition

"be anxious for nothing" is not a condemnation of worry but a prescription for dealing with it.

Dr. Duane Dunham, Professor of New Testament Language and Exegesis at Western Conservative Baptist Seminary, says the verb here is in the present negative imperative and may be translated, "Don't go on worrying."

Paul here admonishes us to resolve our anxieties rather than retaining them. Worry should not be open-ended, a treadmill to nowhere. Indeed, that is the difference between what we might call constructive worry and neurotic worry. Neurotic worry does not lead one to emotional mastery over the perceived threat. Constructive worry does lead to such mastery. Consequently, as we saw in the previous chapter, constructive worry makes one better able to cope with stress.

Starving Birds and Stunted Lilies

Jesus' most extensive teaching on worry is found in Matthew 6:25-34. The passage is simple and yet puzzling. Taken alone, some of Jesus' statements seem to urge a life free not only of worry but of work. "Look at the birds of the air; they do not sow or reap or store away in barns, and yet your heavenly Father feeds them. Are you not much more valuable than they?" (v. 26).

Jesus sounds even more anti-work in his next example: "See how the lilies of the field grow. They do not labor or spin" (v. 28).

It's obvious that the human race could not survive if no one worked, and we have little respect for those who avoid honest labor. We might say, then, that idleness is for the birds.

But does it really serve even them? Though they do not sow seed or store the harvest, they certainly do forage for food. And they work hard to build their nests. Thus their God-given instincts help them provide for future needs, even as we human beings secure our future through forethought.

Most commentators point out that Jesus both precedes and follows his bird and flower illustrations with the admonition: "Do not worry" (vv. 25, 34). He is not teaching laziness or carelessness, they say, but trust. Work is needful—and yes, even foresight—but worry is useless.

Unfortunately, that doesn't quite explain the passage. One major problem remains. Am I not to worry because I see birds and flowers effortlessly prospering under God's care? Fine, but then what am I to do when I see birds starving in a hard winter and flowers choked out with weeds? These things do happen.

Considering the context helps. Jesus tied his worry teaching to a larger principle by beginning it with the word *therefore* (v. 25). What is the previously expressed principle upon which "don't worry" is based? "No one can serve two masters," Jesus said. "You cannot serve both God and Money" (v. 24).

The Lord continually brought people back to the basic truth that God alone must have first place in our lives. We must not be so distracted by other concerns— even for the necessities of life—that he ceases to be our focus. We need to work, to plan for the future, to be concerned about necessities. But always we need to "seek first his kingdom and his righteousness" (v. 33).

What does this passage mean? It teaches the same lesson as does the parable of the seed and the sower, that we are not to allow our hearts to become thorny ground in which the "worries of this life" choke the Word, making it unfruitful (Matthew 13:22).

Worry must never be allowed to crowd out God. But worry does not always crowd out God. It can instead crowd us to God, and that is exactly what happens when we obey the admonition, "Don't keep on worrying, but go to God in prayer" (Philippians 4:6-7).

The End of All Worry Is Not Yet

The Sermon on the Mount, of which the "don't worry" passage is a part, gives the "laws of the kingdom." Matthew's entire work represents the "Gospel of the Kingdom." Whatever your view of the Millenium, it's safe to say that the kingdom of God has not yet been fully established in the world. The meek have not inherited the earth and sin's curse has not been lifted.

Remember that before the curse, life in the Garden of Eden was much like the scene Jesus described in the passage before us. Birds did not have to scratch frantically for food. The lilies of the field did not have an uphill battle against thorns and thistles.

In Eden man lived in abundance. But when Adam sinned, God said that the earth would no longer bring forth its abundance for him as before. Instead he would eat his bread by the sweat of his face (see Genesis 3:17-19).

But back to our passage: When Jesus said not to worry about what to eat because God will provide, he was describing the conditions of the kingdom, a glorious state which has not yet fully come. It is true that sin's curse has already been mitigated, thanks to the blessings of the gospel. Thus the sheer toil required to make a living has often been reduced and the threat of starvation somewhat alleviated.

The curse, however, is still with us. Some birds perish from hunger and cold every winter. Some lilies never bloom. And some people, much more precious to God than birds or lilies, suffer and die from want.

Jesus said that the God who feeds the birds of the air and clothes the lilies of the field will do much more for us. But he still described his own as sometimes having their needs met . . . and sometimes not. Jesus said that he himself, as represented by his people, was "hungry and you gave me nothing to eat, . . . I needed clothes and you did not clothe me" (see Matthew 25:42-43).

The apostle Paul, as one who did seek first the kingdom of God, should have found "all these things"—such as food, clothing, and shelter—provided as well (Matthew 6:33). And generally they were. Yet Paul wrote, "I have known hunger and thirst and have often gone without food; I have been cold and naked" (2 Corinthians 11:27).

So what are the facts?

God is loving and kind. Usually we needn't have any worry about the essentials of life. It is not likely we'll starve. If want does threaten, however, our concern must not be allowed to come between us and our Lord.

How to Worry Well

Paul's prescription for worry is prayer. "Be anxious for nothing, but in everything by prayer and supplication with thanksgiving let your requests be made known to God. And the peace of God, which surpasses all comprehension, shall guard your hearts and your minds in Christ Jesus" (Philippians 4:6-7, NASB).

The very act of prayer, if it is genuine, has profound implications for worry. Prayer brings God into the situation. When God comes in, hopelessness goes out. Though we may be powerless to influence the course of worrisome events, God is not. He can find our lost child, correct our wayward teen, supply gainful work to the unemployed, heal the sick.

He can, but sometimes he does not.

Honesty in prayer surely recognizes that God does not always grant our petitions. We might still have reason to worry even after we've made our requests. So the Scripture goes on to say ". . . by prayer and supplication *with thanksgiving.*"

Here's the critical part: Give thanks. While praying over a concern, I cannot honestly thank God for granting my request if I don't know that he will do so. Sometimes he may give assurance that he will—and in such cases, with the answer on the way, worry evaporates. But in the absence of such assurance, I must either play mind games and try to "claim by faith" what I want, or I must acknowledge that things may not turn out my way.

If I am to thank God even if I cannot thank him for granting my petition, for what shall I give thanks? For past mercies. For his often-demonstrated love. For grace to bear hard times. For who he is.

As I pray and give thanks, my worry is resolved. Not on the basis of a fantasy that bad things won't happen, but realizing that if and when they do, God still lives and will be there with me.

It is said that Martin Luther once went through an extended period of depression and worry. One day his wife came to him dressed in mourning clothes.

"Who has died?" asked Luther.

"God," said his wife.

"God!" said Luther. "How can you say such a thing?"

"I am only saying what you are living," said his wife.

Luther realized he was living as if God were no longer alive and watching over them in love. Immediately, he changed his attitude.

That is what giving thanks will do for us; it will change our attitudes.

The Work of Worry

When real threats confront us, we should work through our worry prayerfully. Doing so includes the following steps:

1. *Face the threat.* Denying real dangers is not an act of bravery but of cowardice. It is not wisdom but folly. And it certainly is not faith; it's dishonesty.

Say, "Father, this is what I'm facing, and it has got me worried."

2. *Reassure the mind.* Though the threat is real, it is also limited. Sometimes it helps to mentally create a worst-case scenario. When you put specifics to the worst thing that could happen in your situation, things come into perspective and nameless horror and dread gives way to, "I wouldn't like it, but I could cope with it."

When you face the threat, you can be reassured with the divine promise, "As your days, so shall your strength be" (Deuteronomy 33:25, RSV). Note that this is no assurance the days won't be awesome, but rather that the grace of God will be sufficient.

Say, "Father, I thank you for putting a hedge about me and allowing Satan to proceed only so far against me. I thank you for your promise to be with me always."

3. *Plan counter-measures.* Almost always one can do something to control or reduce anticipated damages. Think about measures to mitigate pain, limit injury, neutralize opposition, increase your own strength. Approach the trial by thinking, *If such and such does happen, this is what I can and will do.* The panic and sense of helplessness that breed resentment and anger in the non-worrier will not likely overwhelm the one who has anticipated and planned ahead for the very thing that is now happening.

Say, "Thank you, Lord, for the helps that you provide. Give me wisdom and clarity of mind to make the best use of all such helps." Then ask God specifically what to do about each element of the fear you face.

When Jesus Worried

Did Jesus ever worry?

Unthinkable, someone says.

Shortly before Jesus told the disciples to consider the birds and not to worry over what to eat, he was faced with that very issue himself. He had been forty days and nights without food, alone in the wilderness. With his fast over, he needed to eat. How would he ever get back to civilization without some strengthening nourishment?

Satan suggested he turn stones into bread. It was his strategy to focus attention on Jesus' concern for his survival. More was involved than hunger pangs—Jesus had already mastered hunger in fasting for forty days. But he needed nourishment.

If Jesus did worry about what he would eat, however, he did not worry to the point of putting that concern ahead of "the kingdom of God and his righteousness." He refused Satan's suggestion, and afterward angels came and ministered to him.

Whether you believe that Jesus ever worried about food, he certainly worried about the cross. Remember Webster's definition? "Worry: mental distress or agitation resulting from concern usually for something impending or anticipated."

Words could hardly describe Jesus' travail in the Garden any better. Such was our savior's mental distress and agitation that he sweat what looked like great drops of blood while imploring the Father to spare him the impending ordeal of the cross.

But the worry and dread of the cross never came between Christ and his Father. As much as he wanted to avoid the cross, he wanted more to do the will of God. "My Father, if it is not possible for this cup to be taken away unless I drink it, may your will be done" (Matthew 26:42).

Jesus on his knees in Gethsemane is our model for dealing with worry. You and I will never face a worry more wrenching. But we may face concerns utterly devastating to us. When we do, an easy "don't worry" is not likely to help. "Don't *just* worry," is far better counsel, "but urgently take your request to God." He may grant your petition. Or he may summon you instead to a hill called Calvary. If he does, and you agree to go there because the Christ of the cross indwells you, it will be with a heart full of peace that passes understanding.

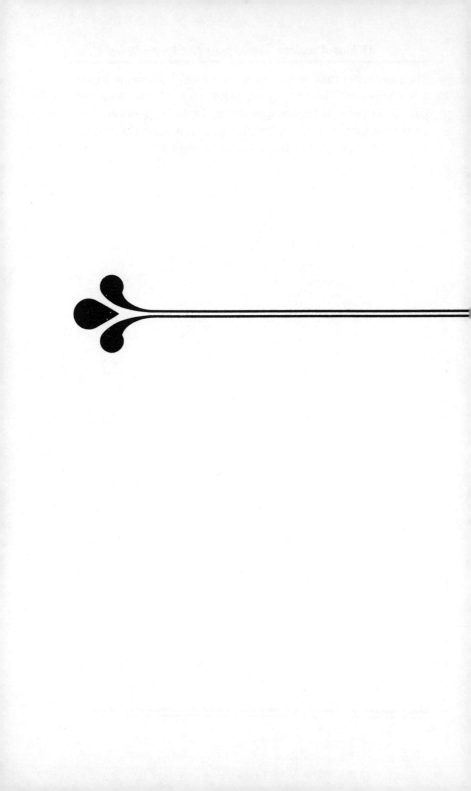

8
When You've Lost Everything

A Rickety Object Lesson

I was driving my family from Three Hills, Alberta, to Portland, Oregon—a distance of about 1,000 miles. Our car was a fourteen-year-old Dodge. Behind us we towed an even older homemade "mobile home." Dodge in those days boasted about its cars' dependability, and for good reason. My Dodge really *was* dependable.

But the trailer was something else.

It simply wasn't roadworthy. The weight was poorly balanced, and the contraption was too heavy both for the tires and for the hitch.

We spent Easter Sunday on the road with this jerry-built rig. Not that we planned it that way. We had intended to be home by Easter. But the spring breakup had left frost heaves all over what had once been a passable highway through the Canadian Rockies. We finally hit one bone-jarring pothole too many, and the steel hitch cracked.

We limped into the nearest outpost of civilization, a dingy and depressing coal-mining town. There we sat until a local garage owner took pity on us and interrupted his holiday long enough to weld our hitch.

Now, if only the tires hold, I thought as we began rolling once again. I had overinflated them to compensate for the excess load, but still they flexed alarmingly. The road was giving them a brutal pounding, too. What would I do if they failed?

"I ought to run that miserable trailer off into the ditch, take our dependable Dodge, and go on home," I said, as much to myself as to Marge. But one thing checked me. That was my frugal (it sounds better than stingy) nature. We paid good money for that trailer, and if we ever got it back to Portland we could live in it.

As I deliberated whether to leave the trailer behind (and thereby lose most of the little we possessed of material value on this earth), a spiritual truth suddenly became very clear. Whether my hitch broke or not, whether I ever got home with that trailer or not, certain secure possessions were mine. God had forgiven my sins and had given me eternal life. Everything in that trailer might perish, but not I. Not I.

A favorite psalm came to mind:

> Praise the Lord, O my soul; all my inmost being, praise his holy name. Praise the Lord, O my soul, and forget not all his benefits. He forgives all my sins (Psalm 103:1-3).

I had noticed before that the first "benefit" the psalmist praised God for in this passage was the forgiveness of sins. David rejoiced in the one asset he had that circumstances could not take away. I had that same imperishable asset.

As it turned out, we made the rest of the trip without incident (of course, the roughest part of the road was behind us). The frustration of that Easter has long since faded, but something from the experience has remained to this day. It is something that provides a wonderful support in tough times.

And what is that? When everything else seems lost, the eternal life that Jesus gives is the one irreducible asset that all believers—including you and I—can cling to.

Now, I realize that my little tale of Rocky Mountain woe might sound trivial to some beleaguered reader. No matter what became of our trailer, we still had our health, our youth, our families, our friends. We weren't even close to losing everything.

But that's typical. People often mistakenly think they have lost everything, or are about to lose everything, when it's simply not true. What has happened?

They've focused on what's lost rather than on what's left.

Some years ago I read about a seventeen-year-old boy in Waukesha, Wisconsin, who killed himself. A newspaper account said he left a note to the effect that, "without my driver's license, I don't have a car, a job, or a social life, so I might as well end it all right now."

Because he had lost his driver's license, he thought he had lost everything. And because he thought everything was lost, he killed himself. As a result, for him, everything *was* lost.

The View from Prison

The imprisoned apostle Paul celebrated what he had in Christ. He didn't focus on his lost freedom. He rejoiced in the same assets of forgiveness and eternal life that encouraged me on the dismal Easter I wrote about earlier. Because of these imperishable assets, his spirit soared even in prison.

Notice this strong theme in the beginning of his letter to the Ephesians. "Praise be to the God and Father of our Lord Jesus Christ, who has blessed us in the heavenly realms with every spiritual blessing in Christ" (Ephesians 1:3).

In "the heavenly realms"? Whatever kind of prison Paul occupied, we can be sure it was no "heavenly realm." Far from it! No, Paul was describing the dwelling places of his soul, not his physical surroundings. He was celebrating the spiritual blessings he enjoyed despite his imprisonment.

As the apostle continued writing, he repeatedly broke into praise for the grace of God. His enthusiasm tumbled out in joyful phrases piled one on top of another. If you have trouble understanding the first chapter of Ephesians, that might be why. One of the important things we teach writers is to make sentences short and simple. Paul forgot all about that as he celebrated his blessings in Christ.

Perhaps it was *because* Paul was in prison that he had time to meditate on the blessings of God until his heart overflowed in this letter of praise. Just so, tough times may prompt us to examine our own lives. They may bring us up short, make us do some heavy thinking. Do we really have any imperishable assets, or not? If so, what are they?

In pondering those questions as they apply to your life, it might help to notice the blessings Paul identified in Ephesians 1 as part of his spiritual inheritance as a Christian.

Chosen, Not Targeted

The first blessing Paul cites is that he was *chosen*. "He chose us in him before the creation of the world" (v. 4). It meant a great deal to Paul that God, before he ever made the earth, looked down through time and chose him. Perhaps the best way to understand how much it meant is to consider the opposite—what it can mean not to be chosen.

It's the feeling you have as a child when your classmates choose up sides to play ball, and you don't happen to play well. The captains start selecting their team members, and of course they choose the best players first. And there you wait suffering. Joe is chosen and Bill is chosen and Bob is chosen, and they go stand beside their captains. The group of not-yet-chosens gets smaller and smaller, until you are left alone. Last of all, because they have to choose everybody, you are taken. "Okay, c'mon, I guess we're stuck with you."

That doesn't exactly strengthen the ego.

The apostle Paul rejoiced because God wanted him. God chose him early, "before the creation of the world" (v. 4).

To be chosen by God is exhilarating. The Jews know that. Down through history they have been honored as God's chosen people. But Paul hints here—and develops later in Ephesians—that there is a new chosen people. Not only Jews, but all who know Jesus Christ are chosen of God.

When things are tough we may be inclined to sneer, "Chosen of God? Tell me about it. Chosen for *what*? I feel more like I'm targeted."

Paul writes, "He chose us . . . *to be holy and blameless in his sight*" (v. 4). Reflect on those words. The King James Version reads, "holy and without blame before Him."

To stand before God Almighty . . . what an image! To stand guilty before *any* authority figure is one of life's harder experiences. Picture a disobedient child taken to task by his father. "Look me in the eye," the father commands, and the child shrivels.

Multiply the intensity of that experience a thousand times and you get a hint of what it would mean to stand, unholy and called to give account, before the God of the universe. Revelation 6:15-17 describes just such a situation:

The kings of the earth, the princes, the generals, the rich, the mighty, and every slave and every free man hid in caves and among the rocks of the mountains. They called to the mountains and the rocks, "Fall on us and hide us from the face of him who sits on the throne and from the wrath of the Lamb! For the day of their wrath has come, and who can stand?"

Would you celebrate, as Paul did, the believer's "spiritual blessings in heavenly places in Christ"? Then just imagine how devastating it would be to stand—tremble might be a better word—before a holy God with your sins unforgiven; and thank him that you will never have to experience such a thing.

God For Your Father

Another imperishable asset Paul appreciated was that God has "predestined us to be adopted as his sons through Jesus Christ" (v. 5). We are not only chosen of God to stand before him holy and without blame, but we are actually members of God's family. We are his children, and we are destined to be fully revealed as such.

Again, this can best be appreciated when we look at the flip side—when we consider what we were by nature. We were children of disobedience and children of wrath (Ephesians 2:2-3). Jesus stated it even more starkly: We were children of the devil!

Paul knew what kind of person he had been, and the thought that God had adopted him greatly blessed his heart. It ought to bless us, too, for when God adopted us we were neither sweet nor lovable. But despite all our ugliness and selfishness, he adopted us into his family.

Being chosen, made holy, adopted—these were blessings Paul enjoyed by grace, blessings the world could not take away. Prison didn't make any difference. The disfavor of the ruling powers didn't matter. Paul had important things and they made his life rich.[1]

In fact, Christ's blessing made Paul's life so rich that he disdained the things he had lost and called them rubbish (Philippians 3:8). The greatest loss Paul ever experienced was probably his loss of standing among his contemporaries when he became a Christian. He described that standing like this:

> If anyone else thinks he has reasons to put confidence in the flesh, I have more: circumcised on the eighth day, of the people of Israel, of the tribe of Benjamin, a Hebrew of Hebrews; in regard to the law, a Pharisee; as for zeal, persecuting the church; as for legalistic righteousness, faultless (Philippians 3:4-6).

Paul was proud of his standing, his reputation, his heritage. We shouldn't scoff at him for feeling that way. Most of us would love to be esteemed of men as Paul was before his conversion. Furthermore, the Scripture says, "A good name is more desirable than great riches; to be esteemed is better than silver or gold" (Proverbs 22:1).

Yet Paul could write, "But whatever was to my profit I now consider loss for the sake of Christ . . . for whose sake *I have lost all things.* I consider them rubbish" (Philippians 3:7-8).

Paul knew how to celebrate when he had "lost all things." He did it by focusing on the greater assets he had gained in the process.

The Richest Man in the Valley

A rich landowner named Carl loved to ride his horse Rajah through his vast estate so that he could congratulate himself on his wealth. One day while on such a ride, he came upon Hans, an old tenant farmer who had sat down to eat his lunch in the shade of a great oak tree.

Hans didn't notice the approaching horseman at first because his head was bowed in prayer. When he did look up, he said, "Oh, excuse me, sir. I didn't see you. I was giving thanks for my food."

"Hmph!" snorted Carl, noticing the coarse dark bread and cheese constituting the old man's lunch. "If that were all I had to eat, I don't think I would feel like giving thanks."

"Oh," replied Hans, "it is quite sufficient. But it is remarkable that you should come by today, sir. I . . . I feel I should tell you, I had a strange dream just before awakening this morning."

"And what did you dream?" Carl asked with an amused smile.

"Well, it wasn't all that clear, sir. You know how dreams are. It seemed there was beauty and peace and music all around, and yet I could hear a voice saying, 'The richest man in the valley will die tonight.' In fact, that was the one part of the dream that was clear, and I woke with those words on my mind."

By now the amused smile had faded from Carl's face and he was frowning.

"I don't know what it means, sir," Hans continued. "Perhaps nothing. But I thought I ought to tell you."

"Dreams!" cried the landowner. "Nonsense!" And he turned and galloped away.

"Lord, have mercy on his soul if he really is to die so soon," Hans prayed as he watched horse and rider disappear.

Carl galloped Rajah only a short distance and then slowed the beautiful Arabian to a walk. *Die tonight?* It was ridiculous, of course. No use his going into a panic. That kind of reaction was what made such predictions come true. If he went galloping like a fool through the forest, he probably would fall and break his neck. The best thing to do about the old man's dream was to forget it.

But he couldn't forget it. Die tonight? How could he, sitting perfectly safe now in his own home? He felt fine. At least he had felt fine until Hans described his stupid dream. Now he didn't feel too well.

For awhile he debated with himself about it, but finally that evening he called his doctor, who was also a personal friend. "Could you come over?" he asked. "I need to talk with you."

When the doctor arrived, Carl told him the whole story. "Sounds like poppycock to me," the doctor said, "but for your peace of mind, let's examine you."

A little later, his examination complete, the doctor was full of assurances. "Carl, you're as strong and healthy as that horse of yours. There's no way you're going to die tonight." He chuckled. "Unless you shoot yourself or something like that."

Carl didn't think his friend's remark was terribly funny.

"Look," said the doctor, "if it will make you feel any better, I'll be glad to stay awhile."

The two friends visited for an hour or so and then played cards through the night. As dawn broke, Carl thanked his friend and told him how foolish he felt for being upset by an old man's dream.

It was about 9 A.M. when a messenger arrived at Carl's door. "It's old Hans," the messenger said. "He died last night in his sleep."

The richest man in the valley had not been the one with vast holdings, but the man of simple faith in Jesus Christ. It's a story to remember when you think you've lost everything.

Losing All the Way Around

Let's face it. I am frankly trying to be as positive as truth will allow. I'm looking on the bright side and hoping my readers will do the same.

I believe my theme, that we can celebrate when things are tough. It's time to admit, however, that not everyone will find it to be true. Sure, Hans could celebrate. Though poor in this world's goods, he was rich in faith. But what of those who have neither the benefits of this world nor the hope of heaven? What of those who are losing out all the way around?

Christina Rossetti caught the pathos of such a sorry state:

> Unthinking, idle, wild and young,
> I'd laughed and danced and talked and sung,
> And proud of health, of freedom vain
> Dreamed not of sorrow, care, or pain.
> Ah! then in those bright hours of glee,
> I thought the world was made for me.
>
> But when the hour of trial came,
> And sickness shook my feeble frame,
> When folly's gay pursuits were o'er,
> And I could sing and dance no more,
> Ah! then I thought how sad 'twould be,
> Were only this world made for me.

If you have only this world, and it turns sour, you are poor indeed. Looking on the bright side cannot help—there is no bright side. No one can—or should—celebrate when things are that dismal.

Still, one hope remains.

Paul wrote of that hope. "For you know the grace of our Lord Jesus Christ, that though he was rich, yet for your sakes he became poor, so that you through his poverty might become rich" (2 Corinthians 8:9).

Did you get that? You can "become rich."

It is actually possible for you, even if you are dead broke spiritually, to open a valid account right now in the Bank of Heaven. A rich man has made provision for his assets to be credited to your account.

It wasn't easy.

He had to go through a personal humiliation to arrange it. But the fact is that if you will apply to God now for a joint account in heaven with Jesus Christ, *your application will be approved.* And you can draw on that account from now on and never exhaust it. You will never be broke again.

How do you open the account? It's simple—just apply to God.

Here's a summary of the account waiting for you:

God so loved the world that he gave his one and only Son, that whoever believes in him shall not perish but have eternal life (John 3:16).

Go ahead. God is "in," and he's ready to take your application.

NOTES

1. Part of this chapter is adapted from the author's book: *What Makes You So Special?* (Grand Rapids: Baker Book House, 1977).

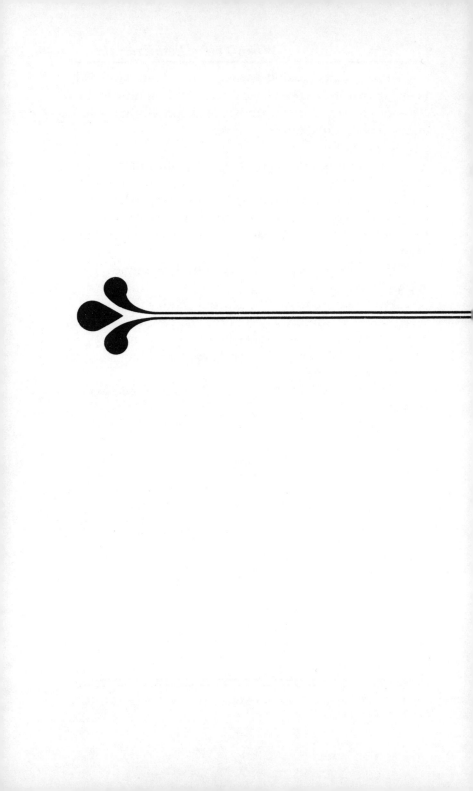

9
When Death Stalks Loved Ones

Why Die?

Today's mail brought two images of death.

First came word that my friend Janice, who had been ill with a debilitating ailment for some months, "goes in for surgery to remove at least five lumps—the biopsies showed malignancy."

Janice is a young wife, a mother of two children, a writer just coming into her prime. Less than a month ago, she called to tell me the happy news that a major publisher had accepted her first book manuscript. Now . . .

I know that cancer isn't always fatal, but the news makes me fear for Janice. *She's too young to die,* my heart protests.

Yet another letter in the mail is from Diana, a young woman I met at a conference only a few weeks ago. She pours out her grief concerning the loss of her son, who died of cancer on his birthday at the tender age of one year. She writes:

> I didn't even know babies could get cancer when our eight-month-old son was

diagnosed with hepatoblastoma—a malignant liver tumor. It was inoperable and the disease had already spread to his lungs. The doctors told us that no child with this type of cancer had been known to survive.

They assured us that the tumor was caused by nothing we had done or had neglected to do. It was neither hereditary nor contagious. Because such a large portion of his liver was involved by the time he was eight months old, they suspected he had been born with the malignancy.

Inwardly, I raged.

Why, God? I thought you took care of infants in the womb. I did my part. I ate right. I had good prenatal care. I prayed every day for the new life forming inside me. We publicly dedicated him to you soon after he was born. *Why?*[1]

The Believer's "Rights"

Diana firmly believed in divine healing. Only recently she embraced much teaching on the believer's "rights." Healing was to be claimed by faith. She concluded that the cancer was God's way of testing her faith, and she determined to meet the test. "God is going to heal my son," she told the doctors and nurses. "You'll see."

For three months Diana refused even to consider the possibility her son might die. That would be a lack of faith. Meanwhile the child continued to deteriorate. He refused all food except breast milk. Diana stayed with him in the hospital around the clock, ready to feed him anytime he would eat. He only grew sicker, and then began bleeding internally.

As I stood by his crib, I poured myself out in prayer and I felt the Lord speak to me. "Let not your heart be troubled: ye believe in God, believe also in me." The words comforted me until I looked them up in John 14 and read the next verse. "In my Father's house are many mansions: if it were not so, I would have told you. I go to prepare a place for you."

Diana resisted the obvious implication of the words. God was going to heal her son. She had declared it to everyone.

The next day the child went into a coma. He never saw the cupcake with one candle that the cafeteria prepared for his birthday. Nor the huge, stuffed green frog the volunteer brought. His body had begun to retain fluids and his tissues swelled like a lumpy balloon. A respirator breathed for him.

Two doctors ushered us into the conference room that evening. "We are doing everything we possibly can," they assured us, and they listed their recent efforts. "He has suffered brain damage by this time and will never again be normal," they said, preparing us for the worst.

"I can't bear anymore," my heart cried out to God. "Why, why, WHY don't you just heal him now? Please God!"

"You must give him to me."

"No, Lord. That would be lack of faith."

Immediately, Diana was struck with the error of her thinking. If she genuinely believed God, she would not try to tell him what to do. She must trust him. "All right. All right. I give him to you," she said.

Diana truly expected that God would now raise up

her dying son. She had surrendered to God, just as Abraham had when asked to sacrifice his beloved son, Isaac. This would now be a tremendous miracle that the medical staff could not deny.

One hour later the child died.

Anger and Confusion

Diana was angry. "Now you've really done it," she complained to God. "For anyone else, I'd ask that you bring him back to life, but you know I can't ask that for my baby after he has tasted the joys of heaven and freedom from pain."

The next days were excruciating for Diana.

> My breasts swelled hard with milk and burned with pain. Medication to stop milk production failed to help. But the physical pain was nothing compared to how badly I hurt inside. It was as though a part of my heart had been ripped out by the roots and I was left bleeding, hollow, aching. I had no idea grief could be so devastating.

Wounded, confused, Diana prayed for daily strength and comfort. At the same time she cowered in fear of another blow. How could she be sure what to expect from God anymore?

A passage in John's gospel impacted her deeply. The disciples were complaining about a "hard saying" of Jesus which they didn't want to accept. Many turned back from following him.

"You do not want to leave too, do you?" Jesus asked the Twelve.

Simon Peter answered, "Lord, to whom shall we go? You have the words of eternal life" (John 6:67-68).

Though her questions remained and her heart ached,

Diana resolved she could not turn back from following Jesus. She simply had nowhere else to go.

Jesus—Our Only Hope

It is ever thus. Because Jesus Christ is within us and there's nothing but a spiritual void without him, we hang on. We get through the hard times. Eventually, blue skies again stretch over our heads, and life is good.

No "answers" will take us through life's hard times. It is not *what* we know but *whom* we know that is critical to our survival. It is Christ who is our Rock. It is in Christ we can do all things. He is the beginning and the end.

And yet . . .

Diana might have suffered less if she had understood more. There are helpful attitudes, and there are harmful misconceptions.

Death Versus the Rights of the Believer

Jesus conquered sin and death once and forever through his own death and resurrection. He defeated Satan and purchased our redemption. Nothing remains to be added to his finished work on our behalf. We must simply claim by faith what he offers us. Satan is defeated, and it is tragic for us to continue to be bullied by him.

All of this is true. The Bible also makes it clear, however, that our redemption is not yet complete regarding our physical bodies.

Perhaps no passage of Scripture throbs with the "rights" of the believer more than Romans 8. From the "no condemnation" of verse 1 to the "nothing can separate us from the love of God" in the last verse, it is a celebration of what it means to belong to Christ.

Yet in the middle of this proclamation of the believer's blessings is a word that some fail to hear.

[18]I consider that our present sufferings are not worth comparing with the glory that will be revealed in us. [19]The creation waits in eager expectation for the sons of God to be revealed. [20]For the creation was subjected to frustration, not by its own choice, but by the will of the one who subjected it, in hope [21]that the creation itself will be liberated from its bondage to decay and brought into the glorious freedom of the children of God.

[22]We know that the whole creation has been groaning as in the pains of childbirth right up to the present time. [23]Not only so, but we ourselves, who have the firstfruits of the Spirit, groan inwardly as we wait eagerly for our adoption as sons, the redemption of our bodies. [24]For in this hope we were saved. But hope that is seen is no hope at all. Who hopes for what he already has? [25]But if we hope for what we do not yet have, we wait for it patiently.

Suffering Now, Glory Later

Observe from the foregoing passage: We *do* experience "present sufferings" (v. 18). We are not exempted from pain because we are Christians. This suffering, we are told, is not only small compared to our future (note *future*) glory, but it is so small as to be not worth comparing. Note too that this all-surpassing future glory is to be revealed *in* us, not *to* us.

Something glorious is going to happen in us because we are Christ's—but it hasn't happened yet! So we wait, along with all of creation, "for the sons of God to be revealed" (v. 19).

We became sons of God when we received Christ as savior (see John 1:12). We are already—right now—God's children. But our sonship is not yet fully revealed.

What still needs to happen for us to be revealed as sons of God? For what change are we still waiting?

The passage answers that question. "We wait eagerly for our adoption as sons, *the redemption of our bodies*" (v. 23).

Our bodies are not yet redeemed. That's why they get worn out and sick, and that's why they die.

Paul wrote elsewhere about this change in our bodies that we await. "We will be changed. For the perishable must clothe itself with the imperishable, and the mortal with immortality. When the perishable has been clothed with the imperishable, and the mortal with immortality, *then* the saying that is written will come true: 'Death has been swallowed up in victory'" (1 Corinthians 15:52-54).

Note the *then,* the future aspect to all of this.

Then "the creation itself will be liberated from its bondage to decay" (Romans 8:21). At the present time, our bodies, along with all the creation, are still in bondage to decay.

That's what happened to Diana's son. That's what is happening to my friend Janice. That's what is happening to you and to me. We all occupy bodies that are in bondage to decay. We are all dying. We can slow the death process, and we should. We can turn back, for a time, the assaults on our bodies. But the outcome is not in doubt.

This might be depressing, but it is the truth.

Jesus said, "I am the truth." He will not deceive us about life in order to make us feel better for a little while. Diana's little while of feeling better, based on false hopes, cost her dearly when the truth proved unyielding.

Nevertheless, we have abundant hope. In a short while our blessed Lord will banish death forever.

But we have something else besides hope; we have

power. As we echo Peter in saying to Jesus, "To whom shall we go? You have the words of eternal life," He replies to us, "I will never leave you nor forsake you." He is always with us, for he indwells us. He will be with us through every battle, including the last one with death. He will stay with us and bring us out whole on death's other side.

How can we say anything but "Thank you, Jesus!"

NOTES

1. Diana Savage Kruger, unpublished manuscript, 1984.

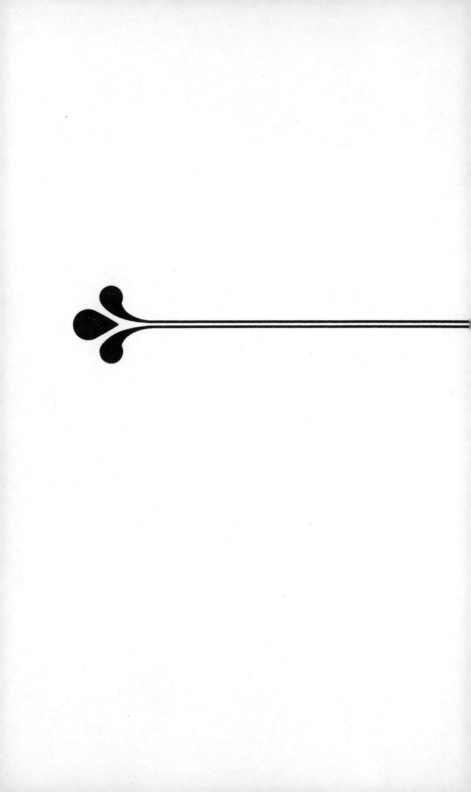

10
When You Face the Last Enemy

Death's Long Shadow

I was seven years old when I had my first personal encounter with death. At Easter, my brother Ron and I each received a real live bunny from our parents, along with a warning: "Be careful playing with them out in the yard. If a dog comes along, it may kill them. So watch out."

I didn't take the warning lightly. My imagination painted a vivid picture of my furry little rabbit being ripped to shreds by the sharp teeth of a marauding dog.

On a sunny afternoon a few days later, Ron and I took our bunnies into the side yard and put them down between us on the grass. We had enjoyed them only a few minutes when a dog trotted by on the sidewalk in front of our house.

"A dog!" Ron cried in alarm.

I jumped to my feet. No dog was going to get my rabbit. I would see to that. I'd chase him away. I took one quick step toward the sidewalk, and my foot came down with all my weight right on my rabbit.

I crushed the insides out of the little animal and I

knew it was as good as dead. That day I got my first demonstration of death's power. Try as I might to defeat it, death had triumphed. My best efforts had not only failed to preserve life, but had destroyed it.

"There's Nothing We Can Do"

I was barely eleven when my father died of Bright's disease. He was stricken on Christmas Day and lay in a coma until December 28, my sister's birthday. I couldn't understand it. He was in the hospital. The doctors knew what was wrong with him. Yet they were letting him die.

"There's nothing we can do," they said. "His kidneys are gone. It's just a matter of hours."

I previously had decided I would be a doctor. That call seemed certain from the day my mother took me to see a doctor for bedwetting and he charged *two dollars* for simply talking with us a few minutes. *Wow, that's for me,* I thought. *What easy money!*

Now I knew that I would never be just another helpless doctor. I would do medical research. I would find a cure for Bright's disease. Nobody should ever again have to hear those despairing words, "There's nothing we can do."

Sin Is the Real Killer

I never became a doctor or a medical researcher. In my teens, I came to know Christ. Then I realized it was sin that killed my father—perhaps directly because his lifestyle aggravated his condition, but at least indirectly because death had entered the world through sin. If I were to fight the real killer, I would have to focus on sin, not on disease. And if I wanted to fight sin effectively, I could best do it by witnessing of Christ, who had already provided the remedy for sin.

Although (or perhaps because) death cast its long shadow over my life early, I have never been able to get used to the idea. I don't understand how some people seem to take death for granted . . . as if it should be expected . . . as if it were *natural*.

My rabbit should not have died; it was all a grotesque blunder on my part.

My father should not have died; it was a failure of medical science, or it was wrong choices on his part, but it was NOT "The Plan." He was only forty-six. I was only eleven. I needed him. His death was just plain *wrong*.

I know that some will say I'm letting my heart do my thinking instead of my head. The food chain depends on one animal eating another, and so does the balance of nature. Furthermore, sheer population control requires death.

I'm also aware that some would say, "Aha! Now we know why you are so religious. You can't accept the reality of death, so you deceive yourself through Christian faith; you make death an illusion."

Death Is Real, but Not Essential

Not so. Death is very real. I have no doubt of that. But why must I see it as essential? The universe has planets like the sands of the sea for number—and I'm supposed to think that population control is an insurmountable problem? Why let my thinking be confined to the circumstances in which nature exists at the moment? God is quite resourceful enough to manage a universe without death.

True, it's my heart that first protests against death as an unnatural intruder into human existence. But my head can grant that possibility as well!

So I continue to protest, although for now death gets the last word. Not every attempt to ward off the dogs of death leads directly to disaster, but something always kills the rabbit. Medical science today has dialysis machines for kidney patients, and can even transplant healthy kidneys into someone who would otherwise die, like my father. But sooner or later, the doctor still tells everyone, "There's nothing we can do."

Realizing Our Own Mortality

We all know we are going to die. It's the ultimate human statistic. One out of every one living person dies, 100 out of every 100, and 1,000 out of every 1,000. (Enoch and Elijah are exceptions, but two out of the earth's billions are statistically insignificant.)

Sigmund Freud and others have argued that we do not grasp that we are going to die and that, in fact, our own death is unimaginable to us. When we think of death, it is of another's death. Or of the death of some part of ourselves.

Existentialists, by contrast, argue that death is the one absolute in life and that confronting the fact of our own death gives reality to life. I am convinced that the fact of our own death is the context in which each of us lives out his or her days. Death overshadows and colors all that we do—even when, as is often the case, denying death is the mode in which we operate.

Why does the teenager want to "live it up" unless he senses that he does not have forever? He not only knows that everyone dies, but he also knows that he personally is on a time track that never can be reversed. He is traveling from birth to death, and anything he misses along the way is lost.

Why must a person get his training, begin his career, raise his family, all in timely fashion? Why does a sense of urgency strike young adults to make them feel they must be executive vice-presidents (or whatever) by the time they are thirty-five?

Why does the person in midlife often face a crisis? He may panic over lack of progress . . . and then despair. Is it not because death is keeping a faster pace than he? Death mocks him and declares that he will never do or be all that he once hoped.

We are in a race and our opponent is death. Time is not the opponent, as we may be inclined to think. Time wouldn't mean anything if we weren't trying to outrun death. We could learn tomorrow, travel tomorrow, play tomorrow, love and work and serve God tomorrow. It's knowing that death will someday deny us another tomorrow that forces us to strive now. We not only may but we must "grab for the gusto." We are not free.

When Hebrews speaks of "those who all their lives were held in slavery by their fear of death," it means all of us (see Hebrews 2:15).

Overcoming the Fear

People fear death because it means an end to their earthly lives. But they also fear it because of what may come afterward. It would be nice to affirm that those who believe in God have little or no such fear . . . yet that is not necessarily so.

Secular studies of how "religion" affects one's fear of death are interesting but inconclusive. Some studies have found religious people are more afraid of death than the nonreligious. Other studies have found just the opposite. Several studies of each kind are reported in "Fear of Death and Dying," by Glenn M. Vernon.

Dr. Vernon suggests a possible explanation for this conflicting data: "Apparently what might have happened to individuals who evidence high fears of death is that, from the whole configuration of 'you are evil—you can be religiously saved' teachings to which he was exposed, the 'you are evil' aspect was given the greatest saliency."[1]

This suggestion makes sense. If what you hear and believe is that you are evil and will face the judgment of a holy God after death, it's no wonder you fear death. But if you hear and believe that you are reckoned perfectly right-eous in Christ and will be welcomed into glory by a loving heavenly Father, fear has nothing on which to feed.

Those of us who minister in the name of God need to ask ourselves which message our listeners are getting. The gospel is a message of forgiveness, of reconciliation, of peace with God through our Lord Jesus Christ. Warnings to the unrepentant and unbelieving are biblical, too, but the salient message for those who respond must be, "Go in peace, you are fully accepted in Christ."

The happy news of the gospel does not at all mean, however, that true believers welcome death. Other factors besides being saved affect our outlook. We still have to concern ourselves with the experience of death itself, and about the termination of our earthly ties and oppor-tunities.

Fulfilling Your Destiny

Sometimes my thoughts about my own death ar-range themselves into a guessing game. I was aware as a young man that, while I could die any day, the chances weren't great. I was at very low risk of death by disease, and only moderately endangered by accidents.

Now middle-aged, I know that my chances of dying soon are greatly increased. I need only look at insurance premium charts to realize it. Rates are perhaps double for a forty-year old what they are for a twenty-year old. They really start climbing at fifty (three times as much) and spurt to ten times as much at age sixty.

But I am me. I am not a statistical average. I have good habits. I don't drink, smoke, or grossly overeat. I'm not excessively driven by ambition. I don't worry much. I know how to handle stress. Most of my predecessors on my mother's side died at advanced ages, as did many on my father's side (excepting the considerable number who opted for hard living).

None of my advantages are guarantees, of course. So when I get sick or sense danger or have pains now, I am likely to wonder, *Hmmmm, could this be it?*

I indulge sometimes in a bit of speculation as to just how and when I will die. Will I outlive most of my contemporaries and die by imperceptible degrees, the last of my generation to check out long after any good reason to live on has disappeared? Sometimes I think that's likely.

But I could be stricken by a fatal disease. Sickness could devastate and ultimately destroy this body that has served me so well up until now. I may have to go through the anxiety of wondering what my disease is, dreading it, hoping it's not serious, and then being disappointed, and all the time fighting to live.

Then again, maybe I will go suddenly in an accident or with a heart attack, leaving family and friends to reel with shock, wholly unprepared for my death. It could happen.

Then again, maybe I will go suddenly in an accident or with a heart attack, leaving family and friends to reel with shock, wholly unprepared for my death. It could happen.

And so I feel like a detective without the clues I need to solve a mystery that will one day be so clear that it will seem the story could hardly have ended any other way.

As I intimated earlier, I didn't view my own death in this almost whimsical fashion twenty years ago. Even now, you shouldn't assume that I'm prepared to go peaceably. Not at all. I'm just somewhat less angry about the possibility of my dying than I used to be.

Circumstances Change Viewpoints

Much of my mellowing attitude can be explained by changed circumstances. Twenty years ago, my five children were aged two through fifteen, and they needed me. Even more compelling than that, I hadn't fulfilled my calling. I had a sense of mission from God—to make my life count for something in his service.

Now the children are full grown, and I believe I have to some degree fulfilled my calling, mostly through writing.

I think I see in Paul a pattern of change similar to what I've just described. He once wrote that to choose between living and dying was difficult for him. "I am torn between the two: I desire to depart and be with Christ, which is better by far; but it is more necessary for you that I remain" (Philippians 1:23-24).

My guess is that earlier, in the first years after his conversion, Paul would have felt differently. Not yet having begun to energetically fulfill his destiny, he would have viewed his death as untimely (see Galatians 1:15).

Late in life, however, he was fully prepared to go. "The time has come for my departure," he wrote. "I have fought the good fight, I have finished the race, I have kept the faith" (see 2 Timothy 4:6-7).

If you are a Christian and have a sense of the call of God on your life, you are probably in one of three states of destiny fulfillment:

You have hardly begun.

You have served the purposes of God for your life but still have much to offer.

You have pretty much completed your work.

You will view your own possible death differently from each of these stages, regardless of your age.

Always an Enemy

Just because Paul was more receptive to the prospect of dying after he had finished his course, it does not follow that he liked the idea. Paul called death an enemy, and he never did change his mind and cozy up to his grim adversary.

Certainly some people desire to die. They say, and really feel, that death would be a welcome release from their suffering. This is not because death has ceased to be an enemy, but because death is winning the conflict and they have lost hope.

Such a person feels that his dying cannot long be suspended, so let it at least come to a conclusion. Let the battle end with his own negotiated surrender rather than his utter defeat.

People speak of dying with dignity, by which they mean under conditions that permit them to influence the way they die, rather than allowing death to entirely humiliate them.

This dying as a last act of defiance can be seen in the condemned criminal who commits suicide. Special precautions are often taken to keep the condemned from taking his own life and thereby "cheating the executioner."

King Saul died by his own hand when the tides of battle turned against him and his death became inevitable.

Death is always our enemy. It is linked in Scripture with two other implacable foes of man: sin and Satan. "The wages of sin is death" (Romans 6:23). "The thief (Satan) comes only to steal and kill and destroy" (John 10:10).

Jesus is our savior from sin and Satan and death. But as we observed in the previous chapter, the redemption of our bodies has not yet occurred. Jesus "must reign until he has put all his enemies under his feet. The last enemy to be destroyed is death" (1 Corinthians 15:25-26).

Experiencing Death

People who have had "near-death" experiences have been the subject of various popular books and television reports in recent years. Most such people, Christian or not, have reported positive, happy experiences.

Helmut Thielicke in *Living with Death* points out that as early as 1938 a French doctor named Barbarin argued in his book *Death As a Friend* that death is a pleasant experience. All the pain and anxiety and turmoil common to the predeath state disappear and the dying person feels euphoric.

Thielicke comments:

> What seems to me to be dubious about the subject matter of these works on the experience of death is the effort to reduce the problem of dying to the last hour of life and therewith to rob it of its character as a sign of our finitude. Awareness of the destiny of death as the constant companion of the whole of life is here suppressed. One might say that the existential character of our dying and our awareness of mortality are eliminated. Whereas death is relevant here only as an event of the last hour, the Christian understanding of death as the "last enemy" has always regarded it as the shadow cast over the whole of existence and as a power that accompanies existence over its whole temporal length.[2]

As we have already observed, death is not only a last-hour phenomenon. Its shadow looms over all preceding life, and it permanently changes whatever existence follows it. Nevertheless, death itself is of interest to everyone, since we must all pass through it.

Reports of pleasant deaths may encourage us, but as

Christians we have something more. I offer as illustration an experience of my own.

A Companion in the Darkness

I was not apprehensive when I made plans to take gas for a tooth extraction. I was happy about the idea. When the soft rubber mask covered my mouth and nose and the nurse-anesthetist began humming softly, I wondered curiously just how long it would take for me to go "out."

A big light shining in my face became my focus as the outer edge of my vision began to darken. The circle became smaller with every breath until there was only a dot of light in the center. And then—total darkness.

Now I'm out, I thought. But the mask remained over my face and the darkness deepened. *What's the matter with her?* I thought. *Doesn't she know I'm already out?* Panic hit me.

This crazed woman was going to kill me!

My mind whirled. *I've got to hold on,* I thought, struggling against the effects of the gas.

"No, I'll hold on to you."

The voice was from Someone closer than hands or feet, and I knew it was the Lord.

I relaxed, and the next thing I knew I was laughing at something I thought hilariously funny. I was coming to and I couldn't wait to ask the dentist, "Are you sure you pulled the right tooth?" My great amusement was an effect of the "laughing gas" anesthesia.

I believe Jesus will be present when we come face to face with death, just as he was with me in that dentist's chair.

Thielicke writes, "We go down into death with empty hands, with no substance of the soul that is sheltered from death, and can only beg God to hold us fast." From our viewpoint, that may be true, but I don't think

we will do any begging. Jesus will be there, even un-
bidden, to assure us that he will never let go of us.

This special presence of the Lord is suggested by the
language of the twenty-third psalm. The psalm talks first
about the Lord. *"He* makes me lie down in green pastures,
he leads me beside quiet waters" (v. 2 NASB). But then
death approaches and the psalmist begins to talk not about
the Lord, but to him. "Even though I walk through the
valley of the shadow of death, I fear no evil, for thou art
(not 'he is') with me" (v. 4).

Killed but Not Hurt

Because the Lord was with him, the psalmist feared
no evil (or *no harm,* as it might be translated). That's beautiful. We may not be able to escape death, but we can escape harm.

Jesus taught much the same thing in a rather curious
discourse to his disciples. In warning them of the persecution they could expect, he said, "You will be betrayed by
parents, brothers, relatives and friends, and they will put
some of you to death. All men will hate you because of me.
But not a hair of your head will perish" (Luke 21:16-18).

Notice: "They will put some of you to death," he
said. "But not a hair of your head will perish."

What's this? We may die but we won't lose any hair?
We won't lie bald in our caskets? Who cares? Frankly,
that's small comfort to me.

But Jesus is really saying that even if we are killed, he
will see to it that we are not in the slightest harmed.

But what does that mean—not harmed?

More Than a Body

I talked with Janice again lately, the friend I mentioned in the previous chapter who only recently learned

she has cancer. She didn't have the surgery to remove the malignant lumps. The doctors said the cancer has spread all through her body and is inoperable.

As the doctors explained the results of their tests and showed Janice the blips indicating cancer in various organs, she had a certain sense of detachment. Her body was racked with cancer, but *she* was deeper. Her body was apparently dying, but *she* would live.

I read this chapter to Janice and to the others in our critique group. "There is much more about death I could say, but my aim is not so much to fully discuss death as it is to help readers get through the hard time of facing death or bereavement," I said.

"I think it's right on target," said Janice. "I've already come to most of those same conclusions. But what is hardest for me . . ." She paused and her eyes glistened with tears. "What's hardest is leaving my family . . . not because of my loss but theirs, especially the children. I don't want them to be bitter because their mother was taken away from them."

Another member of the group, Gloria, cited Isaiah 40:11 (NASB): "Like a shepherd he will tend his flock, in his arm he will gather the lambs, and carry them in his bosom."

"The Lord will take special care of your children, Janice," she said, "and they can become all the stronger for it."

I recalled how, years ago, my Bible teacher had been concerned that his frequent ministry away from home could be detrimental to his children. Once he commented to a friend, "If my children grow up to follow the Lord, it will be only by the grace of God."

The friend answered, "If your children grow up to follow the Lord, it will be only by the grace of God *whether you are there or not.*"

We're Never Left Alone

It is wonderful that Jesus goes with us through the valley of death and out to the other side. But wonder of wonders, he also remains here to tenderly guide and guard those we must leave behind.

So Jesus—blessed Jesus—is the One who will get us through our last hard time. Just as he gets us through every other test.

We may lose everything, but he is still there.

We may not understand his dealings with us and be hurt or angry with him, but he is still there.

We may fail the Lord so grievously that we can hardly forgive ourselves, but he is still there.

We may feel dead inside and have no sense that God is *anywhere,* much less within us, but he is still there.

We may be worried and unable to shake our anxiety because the threats we face are real, but he is still there.

We may be lonely and feel rejected, but he who said, "Never will I leave you; never will I forsake you" is still there (Hebrews 13:5).

We may feel confused and lost because life as we have known it has disappeared and the ground we stood on vanishes, but he is still there.

As long as there is a *you,* he will still be there. And as long as he is there, you will be all right.

"For in him dwelleth all the fullness of the Godhead bodily. And ye are complete in him" (Colossians 2:9-10 KJV).

Complete. Entire. Whole.

He has promised, and so shall we be.

Forever!

NOTES

1. Glenn M. Vernon, "Fear of Death and Dying," in *Sociology of Death* (New York: The Ronald Press, 1970), p. 197.

2. Helmut Thielicke, *Living with Death* (Grand Rapids: Wm. B. Eerdmans, 1983), p. 19.

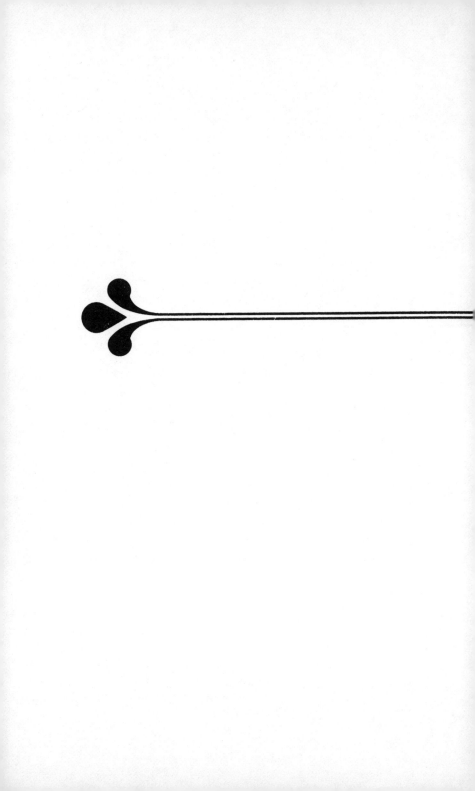

Part 3

Getting Over the
Hurt of Being Human

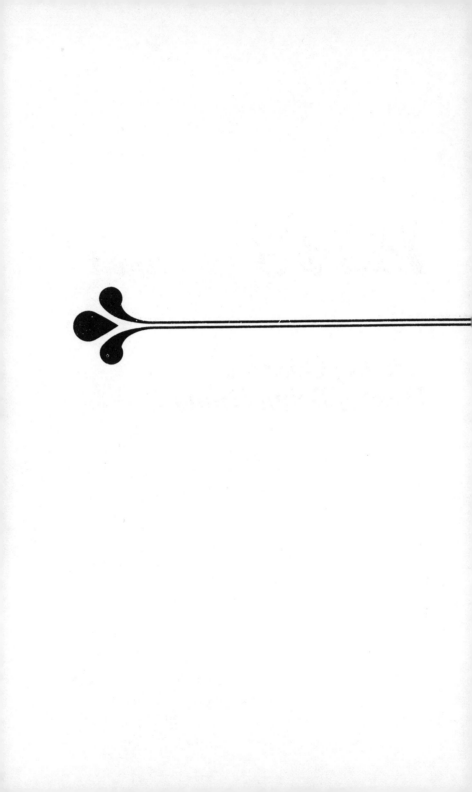

11
When You Have Been Wronged

Gut-Level Hate and Love

One after another they came, people who had been done dirt and who were more than willing to tell about it. I had announced at the close of a singles meeting that I was writing this book and that I wanted to speak with those who had been seriously wronged. As I expected, many of their complaints were against former spouses.

There were the usual: "My husband left me for another woman, and after I gave him the best years of my life."

And there were variations. Joy's husband had left her and their three children after twenty-four years of marriage—not for another woman, but for a man. He announced that he was gay, and though he "loved" his family, he had to go on with his own life. When it all sank in, Joy was bitter. She had been tormented all these years thinking their dismal sex life was her fault. Why hadn't he told her? He had wasted years of her life. She might have found a good marriage with someone else if he had left her at age twenty-two or thirty or even thirty-five. Now she was forty-three years old. Her chances of marrying well were diminished, and even if she did, nothing could restore the lost years.

Cindy had been robbed of her children. She had been a good mother and it never once entered her mind that her husband might win custody of the children when they divorced. Only after it was over did it dawn on her what had happened. Her lawyer was an alcoholic and incompetent. He hadn't presented her case well, while her husband's lawyer had made him look wonderful. The judge, she learned, had himself been divorced and lost his children to his wife. Shouldn't he have disqualified himself? She could appeal, could fight for custody, but that might be very destructive to the children. Cindy simply had no good way out, and she was burned up about it.

Don wanted to make it clear that women weren't the only ones victimized by ex-spouses. His ex-wife had taken him for everything he had. It wasn't as if he earned a good income while she was at minimum wage. She was an executive secretary and made more than he did. What was worse, the home they had owned free and clear—which the judge awarded to her—was his family home inherited from his parents. He had entered the marriage with money and assets; she had not. They had come out just the opposite. "I tell you, there's no justice!" said Don.

Mary asked if I'd heard how some women had worked to put their husbands through college only then to be dumped. When I nodded, she said, "Well, now you've met one."

Not all of the tales of woe related to divorce. Jane was a young widow who felt she'd been wronged by her former church. The other women treated her like a threat to their marriages. The pastor had no compassion. "Your Maker is your husband" he quoted to her from Isaiah 54. The verse was fine but the way he applied it made her feel like she was some kind of sinner for hoping ever to marry again.

Pat, a diabetic, had been mistreated by her doctor. He had failed first to treat the osteoporosis that diabetics tend to suffer. When her toes became so brittle that they broke, he denied they were broken and refused to x-ray them, cursing at her and calling her "a hysterical woman." As a result, Pat has permanently deformed toes and constant pain.

Fred was an abused child. His parents had often locked him in a dark closet for being bad. They yelled at him continually, ridiculed him, and beat him. He grew up like Rob (chapter 2) believing he was worthless but also knowing his parents were cruel. He hated both himself and them.

These were the seriously trampled-upon who were willing to tell their stories. Probably all of us have been grievously wronged at some time, or we will be. When it happens, how do we handle it? What do Christians do when somebody does them dirt?

Getting Even

Darlene Bogle was having problems with her neighbors, the Coopers. They didn't like her cat with its habit of using their yard for a litter box. One day they took matters into their own hands and killed the cat with a BB gun.

An imaginative woman, Darlene disdained ordinary tactics of revenge. She would devise something exotic.

A few days later, the neighbors had no electricity, no water, and no gas. The utility companies had simple explanations. A woman had called, identified herself as Mrs. Cooper, and ordered the services discontinued.

Only the telephone still worked; it had apparently been overlooked. Late that night the Coopers learned why. Someone had placed an ad in the local paper offering their house for sale at an unbelievable bargain price. "Call after 10 P.M.," the ad stipulated.

Darlene remembers all of this with mixed feelings. Now a Christian, she disapproves of her vengeful actions. She knows that Scripture says, "Do not take revenge, my friends, but leave room for God's wrath, for it is written: 'It is mine to avenge; I will repay,' says the Lord" (Romans 12:19).

On the other hand, she still thinks her revenge had a certain imaginative flair. But she now tries to channel her creativity into writing and speaking for the Lord.

Why Not Get Even?

Just knowing that the Lord forbids our taking revenge should be sufficient to keep us from doing it. We want to obey our Lord, whether or not we understand all the reasons for his commands. In this matter, however, the Lord wants us both to obey and to know why.

"Do not repay anyone evil for evil," we read. "Be careful to do what is right in the eyes of everybody. If it is possible, as far as it depends on you, live at peace with everyone" (Romans 12:17-18).

God doesn't want us to do evil. The fact that someone else does evil to us doesn't change that. He wants us to "do what is right," even if others do what is wrong.

As God sees it, and as we need to see it, the problem when we "get even" is that we are doing exactly that. The other person has sunk to a low level, and we are getting down there with him. If our enemy were destitute, would we want to lose our assets too and get even? If he were sick, would we want to lose our health and get even? Of course not. Then if he has done evil, why should we lose our integrity by getting even?

God says in effect, "Don't get even; come up higher." He wants us to be better people.

When we respond to God's command and forsake revenge, we save both ourselves and others a lot of grief. Darlene's actions hurt her neighbors without really helping her, and she increased the likelihood of an even more destructive retaliation from them. As Scripture says, "If you keep on biting and devouring each other, watch out or you will be destroyed by each other" (Galatians 5:15).

If Thoughts Could Kill

You have been wronged. Inside you recognize a desire to strike back, but you won't. God's Word is clear that you must not do so, and you can see some reasons why. You are over the first hurdle—but only the first, for God says you must neither take vengence *nor hold resentment*.

Here's the Scripture: "Get rid of all bitterness, rage and anger, brawling and slander, along with every form of malice" (Ephesians 4:31). Resentment can take various forms and this verse specifically mentions several. Then it sums up all of them with the expression *every form of malice*. That's comprehensive!

This is a good place to observe that "every form of malice" includes resentment toward those who have wronged us in small ways, too. While focusing on serious wrongs, we must not overlook the very real problem we can have over minor slights. The thoughts in this chapter apply to both situations.

But it may be especially different to get rid of our malice when we have been done a *lot* of dirt. Resentment can feel so legitimate. The fact that we can't take vengeance may make resentment seem all the more justified. Are we to let wrong-doers off the hook completely?

Even if we wanted to, we are not sure we could "get rid" of all malice. The feelings are deep. Can a person just tell himself not to feel resentful any more?

Getting Rid of Malice

A number of years ago God and I had to come to terms on Ephesians 4:31. I had some malice I didn't know how to get rid of, and though my complaint may seem minor compared to others, it was a real problem for me.

The church I pastored at the time seemed indifferent to my material needs. If it had been just me, I could have handled it. But I had a wife and family. It was my Christian duty to provide for them. More and more I came under the pressure of a no-win situation. If I stayed at the church, I was depriving my family for whom God told me to provide. If I left the church, I'd be abandoning a ministry to which I felt called by God.

As the situation continued, I felt more and more resentful toward the church. There was no question that they wanted me to stay. Why couldn't they see I needed more money? They knew I had a family. They knew what it cost to live. *I'd like to see them try to get by on my salary* I thought bitterly.

Then Ephesians 4:31 entered the picture. God wanted me to get rid of all bitterness. However legitimate my complaint, God said the bitterness had to go. I noticed that the original Greek expression translated "get rid" was a single word that literally means "let it be removed."

Here was hope—I didn't have to haul my resentment off somewhere. God would remove it. I only needed to let him do so. As I agreed with God on the issue, it was as if a petcock had been opened in my soul and the corrosive acid of bitterness drained out.

Thank God I obeyed the Lord, for otherwise that acid would have continued to eat away at my soul. That's the way with bitterness and malice. It destroys those who hold on to it. Corrie ten Boom saw this in those who suffered the terrible mistreatment of a Nazi concentration camp. She wrote:

Those who were able to forgive their
former enemies were able to return to the
outside world and rebuild their lives, no
matter what the physical scars. Those who
nursed their bitterness remained invalids.
It was as simple and as horrible as that.[1]

In my own case, I still had my underpayment problem, of course, but I no longer resented the people. I was
able to minister to them in the right spirit. Meanwhile, I
considered more seriously whether the Lord might be
leading me to make a change. Ultimately, I concluded that
he was.

The Removal Process

Sometimes it helps to symbolize outwardly our inner
spiritual transactions. To "get rid" of bitterness, to "let it
be removed," you could cup it and dump it, as my friend
Dale Galloway suggests.

Form your two hands into a cup. Now mentally de-
posit all your bitterness, anger, resentment, and ill will
into the cup, along with all the slights and wrongs you
have suffered. Lift your cupped hands to the Lord, then
turn them over, palms down, and dump all the contents
out. Wiggle your fingers so nothing will stick to them. Finally, thank God for removing all that you have dumped
before him.

Feeling Compassion

You have ruled out revenge. You have agreed with
the Lord to give up your bitterness and resentment. By
these two choices, you have won a great victory and severely hampered Satan. He cannot use you to perform destructive acts of vengeance, and he cannot corrode your
soul from within by stirring the acid of bitterness.

You have cleared two tough hurdles. Now comes a third.

Scripture follows up the admonition to "get rid of . . . every form of malice" with the command, "Be kind and compassionate to one another, forgiving each other, just as in Christ God forgave you" (Ephesians 4:32). This means you must now exhibit good will rather than ill will toward anyone who has wronged you.

Gut-Level Love

I'm particularly interested in the word translated *compassionate*. An anglicized form of the Greek here is *eusplanchnos*. The *eu* prefix means *good* or *well* and *splanchna* means bowels or innards. Literally, *compassionate* here means *good insides* or gut-level love.

Deep inside you once had bitterness and resentment. Then you let God remove it. Now he wants you to have—equally deep inside—benevolence instead of malice, good will instead of ill will, love instead of hate.

How do you get this gut-level love?

Just as we needn't strive to rid ourselves of malice, so we don't have to supply love. What we have to do in both instances is to say "yes" to the Lord. In this case we must say, "Yes, Lord, I am willing to have gut-level love toward the person who has wronged me."

As we thus inwardly submit to God's lordship, he sheds abroad his love in our hearts by the Holy Spirit. That's the dynamic behind the well-known gospel song "The Old-Time Religion." One stanza says, "Makes me love everybody," and that is exactly what it does.

Neither the removal of malice nor the bestowal of love is a once-for-all thing. As often as bitterness and hate return, we must come afresh to the Lord for healing.

Learning Gut-Level Love

While God can and will give us his supernatural love for our enemies, the Scripture also teaches that we ourselves should develop brotherly love. "Make every effort to add to your faith goodness . . . knowledge . . . self-control . . . perseverance . . . godliness . . . brotherly kindness . . . love" (2 Peter 1:5-7).

That brotherly love is never more tested than when some brother wrongs us. Two principles will help to keep our perspective straight and our brotherly love operational under such stress. We must learn these principles and learn them well.

1. *We Aren't So Pure Ourselves*

One reason we have trouble feeling gut-level love toward those who wrong us is that there is something of the self-righteous judge in us. We don't like to see wrong-doing go unpunished. When people sin seriously, we think they ought to pay for it. It's not ourselves we are looking out for at this juncture. We aren't asking to be avenged. We just want wrongdoers to receive their proper punishment. Our sense of fair play and justice demands it.

We think like King David did when Nathan the prophet told him how one of his subjects had committed blatant sin. Nathan reported that a certain prosperous man had stolen his neighbor's only lamb, a pet that was like a daughter to him. Though the rich man owned plenty of lambs, he slaughtered and served his neighbor's animal in order to feed a guest.

"David burned with anger against the man and said to Nathan, 'As surely as the LORD lives, the man who did this deserves to die! He must pay for that lamb four times over, because he did such a thing and had no pity'" (2 Samuel 12:5-6).

Nathan replied chillingly, "You are the man!"

David had many wives and could have had more, but

149

he stole the only wife of his neighbor Uriah and then arranged for Uriah to be killed in battle. David was indignant about the wrongdoing of another, but was guilty of worse things himself.

There's an old saying that the pot shouldn't call the kettle black. Sinners shouldn't label other people sinners. Most of us immediately want to reject this argument. "Of course everyone is a sinner," we say, "but we have never wronged anyone as so-and-so has wronged us." We may be convinced it is true and be vehement in declaring it.

Jesus says we are wrong.

It's God Who's Been Wronged

Christ taught that each of us has sinned far more against God than anyone has sinned against us. To illustrate, Jesus told about a man who owed his master a huge debt, more than he could ever hope to pay. The master forgave the man everything. Yet the same man refused to forgive a fellow servant a debt almost insignificant by comparison (see Matthew 18:23-30).

When we maintain that we have never much injured anyone, we forget how much we have sinned against God. We say, "Yes, but they have sinned against God, too, plus hurting us." But that is beside the point. The issue here is our attitude toward those who mistreat us. God's attitude toward us is forgiving even when we wrong him. If our attitude toward those who wrong us is judgmental, we are unlike God and invite his judgment.

This is God's perspective. We can argue if we choose. We can claim a place beside the Holy One and from our judgment seat condemn the miserable sinner who misuses us. We can imagine it is God and us versus the bad guys. But Jesus will have none of that. He says it is wicked to be unmerciful to others when we've been forgiven so much.

Read it for yourself:

Then the master called the servant in. "You wicked servant," he said, "I cancelled all that debt of yours because you begged me to. Shouldn't you have had mercy on your fellow servant just as I had on you?" In anger his master turned him over to the jailers until he should pay back all he owed. This is how my heavenly Father will treat each of you unless you forgive your brother from your heart (Matthew 18:32-35).

Forgive As You've Been Forgiven

Jesus requires that we forgive from the heart, that we exhibit gut-level love. We have been forgiven too much ever to hold anything against anyone else.

It is possible that some readers may honestly not see that they have sinned so grievously against God. But all of us have at times chosen our will over his. We have failed to obey the first commandment: To love the Lord with all our heart, soul, strength, and mind.

Although he made us and sustains us, we sometimes still use what he provides merely to please ourselves—we disregard his desire. We sin against the One to whom we owe everything. By contrast, the sins committed against us are small indeed.

We don't dare be unforgiving. Especially when we pray as Jesus taught us: "Forgive us our debts, as we also have forgiven our debtors" (Matthew 6:12).

2. *Evildoers Don't Get Away with It*

A second reason we don't express gut-level love toward those who wrong us is that we are too busy envying them. The Bible says, "Do not fret because of evil men or be envious of those who do wrong; for like the grass they will soon wither, like green plants they will soon die away" (Psalm 37:1-2).

We often secretly envy wrongdoers, and sometimes the secret is hidden even from us. We don't realize that the reason we are so upset is we're jealous. We'd like to do certain nasty things ourselves, but we fear the consequences. Others go out and do what we'd like to—or something far worse—and get away with it. And we're supposed to show "gut-level love" toward them?

They get their sin and forgiveness too.

A Wrong Perception of Sin

This envy comes from a distorted view of sin's true nature. We fail to see that these people get away with nothing. Sin is both corrupting and destructive. The more a person sins and the worse he sins, the more damaging the results will be in his own life . . . and beyond.

Suppose a person defies the laws of God and man to steal a deadly viper which you had on display. He has wronged you. He escapes apprehension by the law and seems to have gotten away with his crime. Two days later his swollen body is found beside the snake's cage. Is he to be envied?

Sin doesn't always kill people in two days. But if we are anywhere near as godly as we would like to think we are, we should realize that evildoers are to be pitied, not envied. They are stealing poison.

Having gut-level love toward wrongdoers doesn't mean that we wish them well in their sin. It means that we wish them well despite their sin, and we desire that they might be delivered both from their sin and its consequences. The two go together.

A Glaring Contrast

In Agra, India, in 1973, I visited the world-famous Taj Mahal. Though it was magnificent, one of the seven wonders of the world, I met a greater wonder on the same trip in the person of K. M. Usman.

Born in Agra, Usman became the first university graduate of his community and a *maulvi,* or priest of Islam. Eventually he came across a used Bible in which he read some fascinating things about Jesus, who according to Islam was one of the four major prophets of God.

One glaring contrast between Jesus and Muhammad, the founder of Islam, struck Usman. When Muhammad was persecuted, he prayed curses upon his enemies. "Perished be the two hands of Abu Lahab. . . . Soon shall he enter into the blazing fire, and his wife too, who goes about slandering. Around her neck shall be a halter of twisted palm fiber."

Jesus was treated much worse—mocked, beaten, and crucified. Yet he prayed, "Father, forgive them, for they know not what they do" (Luke 23:34 KJV).

Usman marveled. Muhammad's reaction to mistreatment was that of a natural man. Jesus' reaction could be understood only as that of the divine Son of God. Usman was converted to Christ and became an evangelist.

We know that Jesus taught during his life what he exemplified at his death. He said, "You have heard that it was said, 'Love your neighbor and hate your enemy.' But I tell you: Love your enemies and pray for those who persecute you, that you may be sons of your Father in heaven" (Matthew 5:43-44).

Jesus still calls us to be like him in this respect, to forgive our enemies, to be living examples of the divine power of the gospel of Christ.

When we do so, there is no telling who might see it and believe.

NOTES

1. Corrie ten Boom with Jamie Buckingham, *Tramp for the Lord* (Old Tappan, N.J.: Fleming H. Revell, 1974), p. 56, 57.

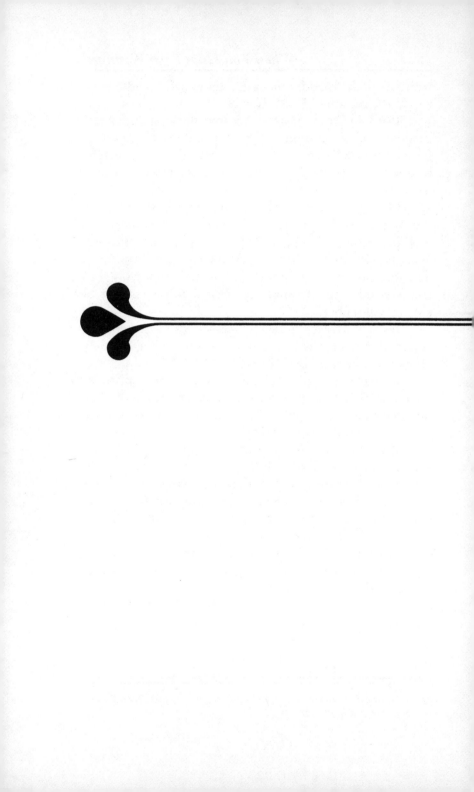

12
When God's Justice Seems Silent

Letting God Be God

Diane Bristol, aged twenty-one, was raped and murdered in 1970 in San Diego, California. Her murderer was eventually caught and sentenced to prison. In 1975 the convicted man, "Tom," received a letter from the parents of the girl. Incredibly, they were writing to express their forgiveness.

More letters and a personal visit followed. The Bristols told Tom about their faith in Christ. They said he could have forgiveness and eternal life through Christ. For a time Tom seemed responsive, but then he ended the contacts.

This was a bitter blow to the Bristols. They had hoped God could use their tragedy, and their witness, in converting the criminal. Though that has not happened, the Bristols still take comfort that God's sovereignty will cause much good to come out of the terrible evil that invaded their lives.

In her book *When It's Hard to Forgive,* Goldie Bristol writes of benefits she has already seen:

I have learned to see God's hand at work through Diane's death. He has used Tom as an instrument to help shave off some rough edges in my life. . . . I know all the deep suffering and anguish my family and I have endured has helped us to grow spiritually.[1]

Some of those seriously-wronged singles described in the previous chapter also said God had used the mistreatment they suffered to benefit them spiritually. Losing material wealth had helped one to get eternal values straight. Losing a companion had helped another to new self-reliance and faith in God.

One of the Bible's most mistreated characters is also one of the strongest examples of how God brings good out of evil. Joseph was still in his teens when sold into slavery by his brothers. Frightened and naive, Joseph wept as he begged those heartless men not to do such a thing. They ignored him.

Years later, Joseph became governor of Egypt. He had power to execute his brothers or to save them and their whole clan from starvation. They feared he would take revenge, but Joseph saw that God had used his brothers' inexcusably wicked behavior for good. He said, "Don't be afraid. Am I in the place of God? You intended to harm me, but God intended it for good to accomplish what is now being done, the saving of many lives" (Genesis 50:19-20).

God Intends and Superintends

To say, as Joseph did, "God intended it for good" is not the same as saying you or I intend something. We intend many things that never turn out the way we'd like. "The road to hell is paved with good intentions," the old maxim says.

But God is sovereign. When he intends something to happen, it happens. God not only intends but superintends. He guides the affairs of man, including man's sins, to eventuate in a happy outcome.

The greatest example of God's superintending sovereignty is the cross of Christ. Peter told those who were party to the crucifixion, "Jesus . . . was handed over to you by God's set purpose and foreknowledge; and you, with the help of wicked men, put him to death by nailing him to the cross" (Acts 2:22-23).

The men who subjected the holy Son of God to the shameful and agonizing death of a common criminal were wicked. Yet God brought eternal life to millions by means of the worst atrocity in the history of the world.

When we've been done dirt, it helps to realize that God not only intends good to come from it, but will superintend the universe to assure such results.

God's Interpreter

Having declared God's sovereignty, we need to acknowledge that trusting in his sovereignty is not so easy when there's no possible plan to be seen and no hint of any benefit to be gained. There are cases like that, both now and from Bible times. Not every "innocent party" story reads like Joseph's.

Think of Uriah the Hittite, the victim of David's plot in the stolen lamb/stolen wife episode mentioned earlier. It's hard to see how God brought any good out of that for Uriah, even though Uriah seems to have been a decent and probably an exceptional man. Indeed, his virtue and strength of character contributed to his death when a less honorable man might have survived.

Uriah's good principles hurt him in two ways. First, they thwarted David's efforts to cover up his adultery with Bathsheba. David ordered Uriah sent home from battle for a brief furlough. He thought Uriah would surely have intercourse with his wife and would then assume that her child by David was his own. But Uriah was so honorable that he wouldn't engage in sex with his wife while his companions were embattled. David even tried getting him drunk to break down his principles. It didn't work.

Second, Uriah's trustworthy character made it possible for David to arrange something really despicable against him. David wrote a letter instructing the commanding officer, "Put Uriah in the front line where the fighting is fiercest. Then withdraw from him so he will be struck down and die" (2 Samuel 11:15).

David sent this letter back to the battlefront by the hand of Uriah himself. He knew Uriah would not steal a look at the letter. I wonder whether David may not have said under his breath, "OK, you righteous dog, you won't even sleep with your own wife, you can just carry your own death warrant to the front."

There was no justice for Uriah anywhere in this account. There was grace for David. He married Bathsheba, and she eventually became the mother of Solomon, David's successor. But Uriah seems forgotten.

Trusting in God's Grace

It is possible that you identify more with Uriah right now than with Joseph. Wrongdoers may be getting all the benefits while you in your integrity get only the shaft. You can't see one thread of good in the fabric of evil around you. If God is superintending everything to bring good out of the evil, you haven't a clue as to how.

William Cowper wrote a well-known poem that applies to such a situation. It begins:

God moves in a mysterious way,
His wonders to perform . . .

The fourth and sixth stanzas of the poem read:

Judge not the Lord by feeble sense,
But trust Him for His grace.
Behind a frowning providence,
He hides a smiling face.

Blind unbelief is sure to err,
And scan His work in vain,
God is His own interpreter
And He will make it plain.

I am not God's interpreter. I can't tell you why his sovereignty permits your mistreatment or how he will work it for good. But I believe that some day, even if it's in the next life, he will make it all plain.

For now, you need to trust God's sovereignty.

You need to let God be God.

Letting Dead Dogs Live

Trusting God's sovereignty is not passive resignation. It is a positive attitude that leads to positive actions. Again we see in David's life a vivid example of this principle. Only this time David was victim, not perpetrator.

Absalom, David's son, had seized the throne and forced David to flee. A man named Shimei stood beside the road down which David and his loyalists were retreating, pelted them with stones, and cursed David for "all the blood you shed in the household of Saul, in whose place you have reigned." He also said that God was judging David for that offense (see 2 Samuel 16:5-8).

This was sheer slander, for David literally bent over backward to be fair to Saul. More than once Saul tried to kill David. Nevertheless, David refused to raise a hand against Saul, even when he had easy opportunity to do so. After Saul's death, there was war between his followers and David's, but David never behaved other than honorably.

Shimei's slander angered David's long-time friend and military commander Abishai, who said, "Why should this dead dog curse my lord the king? Let me go over and cut off his head."

David replied, "My son, who is of my own flesh, is trying to take my life. How much more, then, this Benjamite! Leave him alone; let him curse, for the Lord has told him to. It may be that the Lord will see my distress and repay me with good for the cursing I am receiving today" (vv. 11-12).

We read that "David and his men continued along the road while Shimei was going along the hillside opposite him, cursing as he went and throwing stones at him and showering him with dirt" (v. 13).

Talk about being done dirt!

David believed, however, that God was in control. He even characterized the cursing as ordered by the Lord. He placed his own welfare in the Lord's hands, suggesting that God might be moved to work on his behalf to compensate for the injustice he was suffering.

David's trust in the sovereignty of God gave a constancy to his character. Circumstances change but God doesn't. When David returned to Jerusalem after the defeat of Absalom, he found a much different attitude in Shimei. "He fell prostrate before the king and said to him, 'May my lord not hold me guilty. Do not remember how your servant did wrong on the day my lord the king left Jerusalem. May the king put it out of his mind. For I your servant know that I have sinned'" (19:19-20).

Again Abishai wanted to put Shimei to death for having cursed the Lord's anointed. David said, "Should anyone be put to death in Israel today? Do I not know that today I am king over Israel?" (v. 22).

God had vindicated David. This was a time for celebration and amnesty, not bloodshed and revenge.

No Room for Revenge

So we see that David's trust in God's sovereignty left no room for revenge. There wasn't room when he was down, for God had ordained and would use those circumstances. There wasn't room when he was up, either, for God had enlarged and blessed him. Isn't that good?

Shimei's story also illustrates how persistent evildoers get their just due sooner or later. Though David never retaliated against Shimei, he did tell Solomon about the man's treachery. After David's death, King Solomon promised to spare Shimei so long as the latter remained in Jerusalem. "The day you leave . . . you can be sure you will die; your blood will be on your own head" (1 Kings 2:37).

To this Shimei agreed, but three years later he left the city to track down two runaway slaves. Solomon learned of it, summoned Shimei, and said, "Why then did you not keep your oath to the Lord and obey the command I gave you? You know in your heart all the wrong you did to my father David. Now the Lord will repay you for your wrongdoing" (vv. 43-44). Shimei was then executed.

The Sin You Can Never Forgive

We've said that letting God be God means trusting him to bring good out of evil, whether we can see any sign of that happening or not. It means adopting a positive attitude that sees him at work both when our opponents have us down and when they are at our mercy. But letting God be God means something else that we sometimes overlook: we must not borrow other people's grievances.

There is a sin you can never forgive, and that is the sin committed against someone else. You can't forgive it because you aren't the one wronged. Since you can't forgive it, you also must not "buy into" it. In other words, it is not your place to resent or revenge a wrong done to someone else (unless you have been given authority in the area). That is God's place, and you must let God be God.

Imagine with me the following scene as it might have occurred in the strategy room of Satan, the prince of darkness.

A Counsel of Darkness

"I hate meetings like this," whispered Stenchsmell as he leaned toward the fastidious figure in the next chair, jabbing his finger at the line on the agenda that announced the purpose of their meeting.

Meanmind leaned away and tried not to breathe. "Yes," he hissed, "It really stinks!" *What an incredibly clever reply,* he thought, but it was one only he would appreciate. Old Stench was as stupid as he was obnoxious.

"The meeting will come to order," said Satan, and the room became silent. "We have a task of the utmost difficulty," Satan continued. "The question before us is: How to destroy the virtuous types who seem immune to our usual vulgar tricks."

Slubgub, who sat across the table from Stenchsmell and Meanmind, stirred slightly in his chair. Pausing uncertainly after every other word, as he always did, he said, "I think—I think—I may—have stumbled—onto something—your infernal majesty."

"Stumbling would be the only way he'd get on to anything," murmured Meanmind.

Satan rapped his gavel and shot a warning look at Meanmind. "Yes. Continue, Slubgub."

"I don't know—if you'll—if you'll—if you'll--like the idea."

"Well, you never will know unless you tell us about it, now will you?" sneered Satan.

"Hmm—ah, okay—but you—but you understand —it's just—it's just—it's just—a suggestion."

Meanmind drummed the table with his fingers while Stenchsmell, in a forbidden moment of forgetfulness, rolled his eyes toward *heaven*.

"Tell us your accursed idea!" roared Satan.

"It's spelled—it's spelled—out here," whimpered Slubgub, offering copies of a memo to each member. At the top was a heading: "The Slubgub Principle," and underneath was a case history.

> Date: The year of our Enemy 1984
> Place: Scudderville, Tennessee, U.S.A.
> Category: Pastoral fight: Fourth Baptist
>   Church

> Following standard procedures for sowing discord among brothers, I prompted the dismissal of two successive pastors, each of whom had considerable potential for aiding the Enemy's cause. I accomplished this despite strong opposition from a disgustingly spiritual and high-principled group of the Enemy's followers. In the midst of my campaign against yet a third pastor, I reaped a bonanza. I noticed that the righteous people, the ones opposing my work, were developing a strong sense of indignation against those I was using to oust the pastor.

> At first I didn't recognize what a marvelous opportunity that afforded me. You see, these people were the Enemy's delight and were extremely hard to subvert. Our agents had tried, believe me, but they had resisted our best ploys. Even when we incited somebody to hurt them, they followed their Master's sickening example and actually forgave those who wronged them.

At this point the reading was interrupted by a chorus of boos and groans from around the table. All were united in their revulsion. Then Slubgub continued:

> When the third pastor was ousted, these good people said they'd had enough. They denounced those I had used. They split the church. I must confess that my joy at the split was marred at first by the fear of what the new church might do to our cause.
>
> I needn't have worried. They were too filled with self-righteous animosity toward their old adversaries to do much for the Enemy.
>
> That's when I saw it. If we can get people to resent the way someone else is treated, we've got them. From a sense of fairness and love and loyalty to the wronged one, they nurture hard feelings toward the ones who have done the wrong. How's that for using good to do evil?

An Old Tactic

Satan put down the memo and a smile flickered across his lips. But only for a moment. "You fools!" he raged. "I invented this tactic long ago. Why haven't you been using it more?

"The Slubgub principle, indeed! This is straight from my old Absalom file. You devils need to study your manuals.

"Since you are so ignorant, I'll refresh your memories." Satan began his story, telling it with obvious relish. "Absalom was a disgustingly beautiful person, once. He was a son of that man I hated so, David. Absalom posed a serious threat to me, for he was a real charmer and could have led the people after the Enemy to a degree I don't even like to think about.

"I made him mine, though, by the same tactic Slubgub here vainly imagines he has discovered. I destroyed the good man by making him hate a bad one—for a wrong done to someone else.

"Amnon was our man," Satan continued. "What a delight he was! Truly a vile, treacherous, low little weasel. He lusted after his half-sister to the point of feigning illness. He lured her into his room under the pretense of needing her care, and then forced her into sexual intercourse. After that, he ignored her pleas that he marry her to save her from disgrace.

"It was a real victory for us," said Satan, "and the best was yet to come. Absalom was outraged by what Amnon had done to his sister. I stoked his fires of "righteous anger" for two years until Absalom could kill Amnon without a twinge of conscience. In fact, he felt proud of it. Absalom became ours, and all his potential for leadership came with it. I even came close to destroying David!"

Damage Control

Although the scene I have described is imaginary, the church split and the murder were actual. (The church name and location are fictitious.) If we are to avoid adding evil to evil and falling prey to the wiles of Satan, we must resist the inclination to hate those who wrong others. We must leave the judging to the Lord. We must let God be God.

Being done wrong is a little like coming down with the measles. At best the measles are a miserable thing to have to endure. The more serious danger, however, is in the complications that may follow—inflammation of the brain, impaired vision, pneumonia. German measles can even damage one's unborn child.

If you've been seriously wronged, beware of a mind inflamed with anger, of vision so blurred that you can see neither your loving Father nor the other person clearly, of an inability to breathe free. Most insidious of all, beware of causing unseen damage to your children, including those yet unborn.

The wrong you have suffered is bound to be distressing; but it doesn't have to be disastrous. It can be turned into victory through the power of the indwelling Christ.

This Christ is the One of whom it was long ago prophesied that he would crush the serpent's head even as the serpent was striking his heel (see Genesis 3:15). The crucifixion of Jesus was the serpent's strike. But Christ delivered a final blow to Satan's head through that same cross.

The serpent, writhing in death throes, still strikes at the heels of Christ by sinking his venomous fangs into his people. His fangs may be piercing you even now.

But take courage!

"The God of peace will soon crush Satan under your feet" (Romans 16:20).

NOTES

1. Goldie Bristol with Carl McGinnis, *When It's Hard to Forgive* (Wheaton, Illinois: Victor Books, 1982), p. 161.

13
When You're All Alone and Blue

Sometimes Lonely Is a Good Thing

In August of my eighteenth year I set out alone to climb Mt. Hood. It is dangerous (at best) to climb Mt. Hood in August, because at that time of the year the perpetual snow fields on those steep slopes become unstable. Solitary and inexperienced climbers invite disaster.

Nevertheless, I drove to Timberline and spurning the trails beginning there, headed straight up the mountain toward its peak. "The shortest distance between two points is a straight line," I told myself.

No one knew I had gone to the mountain and I didn't bother to register at Timberline Lodge as a climber. If I had gotten into trouble, it was almost certain no one would find me in time to save my life.

Far up in the snow fields I found my ascent blocked by huge crevasses. These cracks in the ice were a hundred or more feet long, four to ten feet wide at the top, and narrowed as they plunged into blue-white depths. They also veered off at an angle as they descended. I could not tell how deep they were; it could have been 40 feet or 400.

Either way, a fall into one would mean the end.

At first I skirted a crevasse or two and kept on climbing, but I soon encountered more and more of them. So much for my straight-line-between-two-points theory. I turned to survey what seemed like the whole world at my feet. Far below, the massive lodge at Timberline looked like a child's toy. I knew no one there could even see the tiny speck on the mountainside that was me. I was absolutely alone in a world of white.

I can hardly imagine a picture that better bespeaks loneliness than an isolated figure in the middle of a vast mountain snow field. But things are not always as they appear. I was not lonely in an unpleasant sense. I felt something exhilarating, something glorious about being there.

For a few moments I drank in the splendid solitude. Then, aware that this place was not only awesome but potentially deadly, I reluctantly began my descent.

Alone Is Not the Same As Lonely

My solo visit to Mt. Hood should tell you something about me. I like being alone, going fishing alone, hiking alone, working alone. "I enjoy my own company," I say with considerable satisfaction.

On the other hand, I definitely do not enjoy being alone in a crowd. For much of my life I had felt alone in a social gathering, especially an unstructured one. I didn't mix well. The superficial chatter made me ill at ease. The talk was usually frivolous and the whole atmosphere phony. I didn't care to compete for the floor and didn't know how. So I escaped by saying, "If others want to talk so badly, let them, even if they don't have anything to say."

I learned early that being alone and being lonely are not the same thing. Since then I've learned a few more things about loneliness. There are at least three different kinds of loneliness, and they have different causes. When this is not understood, we often try to apply solutions to our loneliness that have nothing to do with its true causes. That doesn't help, of course, and it *can* hurt.

The Loneliness of Individuality

A certain loneliness is essential to one's individuality. Let me illustrate by citing three examples—one from my personal life, one from recent history, and one from Scripture.

We live in the country, and in the summertime I like to go out at night and gaze at the sky. I watch the lights of passing airliners as they seem to play among the myriad stars. I know that directly above there are perhaps 100 people bound for Portland or San Francisco, all of them oblivious of me. I see the moon, full and luminous. I hear the croaking of frogs in a nearby pond as they fill the night air with music, stopping in unison as if led by an invisible conductor.

Because nobody shares the beauty and wonder of the moment with me, I feel lonely. And then I realize that no one can share it. No one, however close to me, could participate in my awe. Talking about it would only mar the vision. But unless we communicated, we would simply be two people standing there, each one alone, neither knowing the deep wonder (or lack of it) in the other person.

I alone enter fully into the inner thoughts and feelings of my heart. The only way I can escape this loneliness is to stop thinking and feeling. To stop *being*.

The Shadow of a Machine

This "existential loneliness" involves much more than experiences of moongazing. I am alone, too, in my calling from God. No one else can answer with me concerning the purpose and meaning of my life. God is shaping me to be an individual fit for eternity, and the process is essentially One-on-one.

If I do not understand and accept this, the loneliness may become too much to bear. To escape the responsibility of this loneliness I may forfeit my very identity.

Thomas Edward Lawrence, better known as Lawrence of Arabia, rose to near-legendary fame in the early twentieth century. Born in Wales and educated at Oxford, he became a hero of World War I as leader of the Arab forces fighting on the side of the Allies. Wearing a robe like an Arab and riding a horse, he confounded the opposing Turkish forces and fired the imagination of the western world.

His identification with the Arabs became so great that he resented what he saw as their mistreatment by his own British government. He therefore refused medals of honor from both Britain and France. Yet his lonely efforts on behalf of the Arabs ultimately proved futile.

Lawrence was disillusioned. He fled his world-wide fame and abandoned his colonel's rank, changed his name to John Ross and enlisted in the Royal Air Force as a private. When exposed, he adopted yet another name, T. E. Shaw, under which he served in a lowly rank the rest of his life.

At age forty-six he was discharged from the military, an empty man who spent his time puttering around as if "there is something broken in the works . . . my will I think" (Encyclopedia Britannica). Soon afterward, he died in a motorcycle accident.

Concerning his choice to become an obscure enlisted man, Lawrence had once said, "I do it in order to serve a mechanical purpose, not as a leader, but as a shadow of a machine. . . . It is a blessing to be only a part of a machine."

To bear limited responsibility, to become an anonymous cog in an impersonal machine—it seemed wonderful to Lawrence. By biblical standards it was a tragedy. The blessing of God moves in just the opposite direction, calling us to more and more individual responsibility.

As Jesus phrased it in his parable of the talents, "Well done, good and faithful servant! You have been faithful with a few things; I will put you in charge of many things. Come and share your master's happiness!" (Matthew 25:21).

Lawrence didn't want to be "in charge of many things."

It's entirely possible that someone reading these lines may feel the same way. You may be overloaded with responsiblity. You seem to detect an absolute contradiction between the two concepts Jesus joined together. "In charge of many things" doesn't fit with "share your master's happiness." To you, "In charge of many things" equals unbearable strain.

There are many ways to relieve an overload: Get strength from the Lord . . . take better care of your body . . . find restful diversion . . . eliminate some less important stressful responsibilities. You might even withdraw from the arena temporarily.

But whatever you do, don't forfeit your calling. (This forfeiture is described under other terms in chapter 5, "When Comfort Is Worse Than Pain.") Don't give up and bury your talent. To do so is to choose a puttering, something-broken-in-the-works existence.

The Lonely Jesus

We have been describing the loneliness we must bear as individuals. Presently we will consider a third example, one from Scripture, which will bring into view another kind of loneliness. It is a loneliness we need not and should not bear, seeing that we are members one of another.

Then Jesus went with his disciples to a place called Gethsemane, and he said to them, "Sit here while I go over there and pray."

He took Peter and the two sons of Zebedee along with him, and he began to be sorrowful and troubled. Then he said to them, "My soul is overwhelmed with sorrow to the point of death. Stay here and keep watch with me."

Going a little farther, he fell with his face to the ground and prayed, "My Father, if it is possible, may this cup be taken from me. Yet not as I will but as you will" (Matthew 26:36-39).

Jesus took His disciples with him to the garden. Once there, he took three of them aside to support him in his great sorrow by both their physical presence and their prayer. This remedies one kind of loneliness. When we need human companionship, it should be there for us in the community of believers.

Notice, however, that Jesus separated himself even from these three closest friends when he fell face down alone as he poured out his soul to God. If you read on in the passage, you see that while he agonized in prayer, they fell asleep. That's how alone he was emotionally. Care as they might, and try as they would, there was simply no way the disciples could fully enter into the experience our Lord had to endure.

Those, then, are my three examples. I was alone in my awe of the starry heavens. Lawrence of Arabia, unwilling to continue alone as a leader, surrendered to an existence of mechanical puttering. Jesus agonized alone in Gethsemane even though his closest disciples were with him.

So it is with us. We are essentially alone. The famous Antarctic explorer Richard Byrd once survived for five months in a nine-by-thirteen foot hut, isolated in the frozen wastes some 123 miles away from the nearest human. He later related his experience in a book with the cryptic, one-word title *Alone.* Our individuality makes *alone* the name of everyone's book, yours and mine included.

The Potential for True Companionship

There is great loneliness in our individuality . . . but also the only potential for true companionship. Two or more people truly sharing life is the essence of togetherness. But you can't have this sharing unless you begin as separate entities. There can be no communion between shadows, no camaraderie between parts of a machine. We might say that *two requires one.*

If that's true, what are our choices?

We can accept the intrinsic loneliness of being individuals and the result (at least potentially) will be the non-loneliness that comes from true companionship with others.

Or we can flee from this loneliness—and doom ourselves to a desolation without true companionship. Two cannot come together unless each one first exists separately.

This principle—that relationship depends on individuality—applies to God as it does to man. Nobody ever came to God except as an individual. It is on that One-to-one basis that the Lord Jesus Christ calls us. He says, "Here I am! I stand at the door and knock. If anyone hears my voice and opens the door, I will come in and eat with him, and he with me" (Revelation 3:20).

That is companionship!

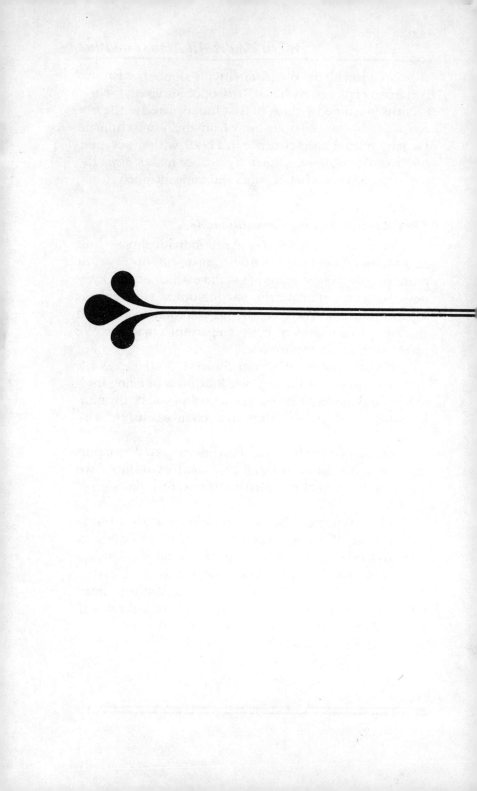

14
When You Feel Isolated and Rejected

The Loneliness No One Should Have to Bear

A few months ago we acquired a pet duck. On her first day at our place, she got out and followed a neighbor girl who was walking past on her way home from school. The duck stayed at the girl's home all night and the next morning followed her back to our place. If we had not seen the comical pair as they passed, I suppose the duck would have followed her to school.

The duck soon learned to stay close to home. She loved the frog pond, and was perfectly content there as long as someone was with her. Let us head for the house, however, and there came the duck at full waddle, trying to stay at our heels.

As she grew older "Quack Quack" (as I called her) didn't seem quite so eager for human company. She didn't always follow us. She began risking her very existence waddling around almost under the hooves of two horses in a nearby pasture. When the horses sometimes departed for greener grass, Quack Quack lived up to her name as she called desperately for her enormous friends.

That silly duck would risk her life rather than be alone.

The Loneliness of Isolation

We said at the beginning of the previous chapter that three kinds of loneliness exist. We dealt at length with one, the *loneliness of individuality*. We also touched on a second, the lack of companionship. We can call this the *loneliness of isolation*.

Abating this loneliness requires us to mix with other people, though we must remember true companionship will develop only to the degree that we (and they) avoid becoming "shadow people."

Nevertheless, there seems to be a loneliness almost biological in nature (as our duck attests). The entire animal kingdom demonstrates it; beasts do not like to be alone.

Like the animals, we may find almost any company preferable to none. Still, we often feel quite isolated and lonely if we lack quality interaction with our own kind.

A mother of small children has company enough, to be sure, but she still may long for another adult with whom to relate on an equal plane.

An older woman may have a large, extended family, but even if she lives in a rapid boil of activity, loneliness may stalk her and cause her to wish for a companion who would call her something other than "Grandma."

A single person can work with others all day, can mix socially and be involved at church, and still be desperately lonely. Flo Bryant, a Chicago-area nurse, was such a person. I first heard of Flo when, after reading a couple of my books, she wrote to ask what other books or tapes might be available. I replied, and some months later she wrote again. With her permission, I now relate the subsequent correspondence.

I'm writing to you once again to ask some questions. Maybe you can help me. If not, that's OK also 'cause I have been needing an answer for a long time.

Have you any advice for someone depressed? I have tried to talk to several people and all I hear is "it will pass." It hasn't.

I realize you are busy and it's OK if you don't have time for this. I know somewhere there is an answer. I just haven't found it yet. But I am desperate.

It's funny, but everytime I read the first pages of your book *Love, Acceptance and Forgiveness* I cry as if I had never read it before. I've never been so alone in my life as now. And, yes, I go to church every week. But it has not got what you talk about. I haven't found a church yet like you describe. If your church is like that, then the people are lucky.

Tell me, is something wrong with me to want a hug once in a while? I don't mean anything sexual. I mean a Christian hug or a touch on the arm. I can't remember when I've ever been hugged at church.

I'm depressed to the point I think death is a release. Now before you think I'm going to do anything, I'm not. But I would really welcome the release of this hell inside of me. I am at the crossroads of my life and I don't know where to go.

I believe in Jesus, I really do. But at times I need something more, if you know what I mean. This is not life. Each day is a battle to keep going. When I drive my car,

I have to be on top of myself because I find I take chances.

Pastor Baldwin, I don't know what to do. I have done all I know to do but it's not enough. Do you have any suggestions on how to fight depression? Any tapes I could buy? Anything?

The urgent tone of the letter prompted me to reply immediately. I assured Flo that nothing was wrong with her wanting a human touch or a hug. I said, "At our church and many others, the people hold hands while we pray." I suggested some books on depression for her to read and urged her to get counseling. I was also able to speak words of assurance to her from the Lord, because I sensed that she was his child and potentially complete in him (Colossians 2:10).

After many months I received a third letter, written on some positively delightful "happy" stationery. On the envelope was a heart-shaped sticker that read, "The difference in me is Jesus." Inside was a quote attributed to a J. A. Holmes: "There is no better exercise for the heart than reaching down and lifting someone up." The letter said:

I found your address and wanted to write you just because. No earth-shaking deal. Just me telling you that in the process of growing there is much pain but the end product is there.

I'm going to a Bible study on Friday where there are lots of hugs for everyone, plus some kisses for the cheeks. Where I go to church the touching is out, except for a handshake when you leave. I never knew what I was missing until I read your letter and I went searching.

I have to be honest. There is one big reason I'm still alive. For me to take my life is a sin. Every time I think about life and death, I have to measure the outcome, and as a result I'm still alive. But now I've taken some steps to help myself. I read a lot, especially the Bible. I'm going to a Christian counselor. I don't really think much has been accomplished, but I guess it all takes time.

But most of all, I'm discovering God's love. At times I just know I don't fit, and then gently I'm led to Colossians 2:10. I know that I am the only one, with Jesus, who can change myself. The sad thing is, though, I tried so long to discover God's love.

Nothing will ever change my ideas about God's love. Nothing. I still believe the end result of all the grief and heartache is healing.

I have a nurse who really has disliked me for a long time. She has even tried to get me fired. I finally had to tell her it was OK if she didn't like me, it was her problem. My problem is what I am doing about it. I don't know what I've done to her but I asked her forgiveness. She says she can't remember, just that she is mad at me. So I made it a weekend of reading and praying and asking God to help me love her. He did. Nothing has changed, but I have. I still get cut down by her and it still hurts, but it's OK.

I just need to learn more about God's love and forgiveness. Then I'll be even more better.

Well, bye, and take care. I've not met

you but I consider you my friend. Thanks.

There was one more letter. I wrote to ask if I might share her correspondence with you and she replied:

Your letter got me thinking of the ways I've been helped. For so long there really was nothing in the way of people to help. There were books, but so many said a lot of nothing.

When I wrote to you, reason told me you couldn't help, but you did by listening. I needed badly some weeks ago to talk to my pastor, and because they are in meetings, he said he was busy and it would have to wait. But, you see, I couldn't, and sometimes death doesn't wait either. So that is why I write from time to time, because even if you can't talk to me your letters tell me I'm important enough to write to.

You had suggested my going to a counselor, which I've done. I was given a test about a month ago. Do you know what it revealed? I was 90% depressed, 100% hostile, and very much submissive and ready to break. He said I was heading for a breakdown or suicide.

I have realized what I was choosing and each day it is a battle to keep going, but as you see I am still here. I'm still moving on because out of all the darkness I believe in God's love. And I learned it from books like yours. Pastor Baldwin, do you know for many like me this is the only way we get love?

In my job I've discovered I'm very able now to fully reach out and touch my pa-

tients. For the first time in months, after I
left a patient's home, I cried because she is
eighty-one and dying of cancer. I found I
really did care and the tears were real. I
finally broke through the wall a little and
it's a beginning.

There is so much in these letters, but I'll not attempt
to analyze them in order to point it all out. It is enough to
say that a once lonely, isolated, and hurting person has
been touched with the love of God. And she will soon be
touching others with that love.

The Loneliness of Rejection

There is a third major kind of loneliness. It is associated with and caused by rejection. We are likely to experience this loneliness when we are rejected by any of the
people especially close to our hearts, even if we still enjoy
acceptance by others.

Jennifer taught a women's Bible class and served as
an officer in the women's fellowship of her church. Her
husband left her for another woman, and over the next few
months she was dismissed from all ministries at the
church. The leaders said they didn't blame Jennifer for the
breakdown of her marriage. They said they would stand
behind her. But they also said she "needed time" and it
wasn't "appropriate" for her to continue in leadership.

Jennifer had heartache enough dealing with her husband's rejection—and now to feel rejected by her church
as well! "We're standing behind you," they told her. But
what did that mean? No one seemed to understand. No
one seemed to be with her. She felt desolate, alone, resentful of her rejection and guilty for that resentment.

Jim lost his job and couldn't find another. As long as
he lived, he would never forget the humiliation he felt
when he was laid off. To lose his job was bad enough, but

the insensitive way it was done . . .

One Friday at quitting time, some clerk from the office stood at the time clock handing pink slips to everyone who was being "let go." With a smirk on his face, he said, "We won't be seeing some of you fellows around here anymore."

It tore Jim up inside every time he applied for a job and didn't get hired. How desolate he felt as he walked away after each unsuccessful try, a curt "Sorry" chewing at his gut. The loneliness plagued him even as he read the want ads and saw others heading for work in the morning or returning home in the evening.

Like Jennifer and Jim, I too have experienced the loneliness of rejection. Many years ago someone I counted a friend turned against me. It came at a time when I was down already and facing severe trials. When I learned my friend was slandering me, it was almost more than I could bear.

Yet experiences like mine and Jennifer's and Jim's are mild compared to the long-term rejection and loneliness some face. Think of the lepers of biblical times, cut off from family, friends, and community. They cried, "Unclean, unclean!" to warn people away.

Think of forgotten prisoners of our own times, long since abandoned by what family and friends they ever had. Think of the deformed, who cannot be seen without a shudder of revulsion by those blessed with normal appearance.

Think of those disgraced in public office, once people of power and prestige, but now reviled.

Talk about lonely.

What to Do with It

Sometimes we over-react. When we read total rejection and personal condemnation into conditions such as being unemployed, divorced, criticized, or set aside from ministry, we may be over-reacting. Not only is loneliness eating at us, but so is self-pity.

On the other hand, I would never try to dismiss your anguish just because others have it worse. A common fault among Christians is to fall short of the love for neighbors that Jesus commanded us to practice. You very well may have suffered because of that fault.

The critical question, however, is not whether your feelings—and the treatment that provoked them—are justified, but what can you do about it?

The Strange Effect of Pets and Plants

Remember my duck? She craved my company or the horse's company—*anything* rather than being alone. Rejected and lonely people have found they, too, can get great solace from other living things when they are cut off from human companionship.

Some sense it intuitively. Whittaker Chambers went through a long and painful ordeal in the late 1940s. He was the chief witness in the government's attempts to convict state department official Alger Hiss of being a Communist spy. Chambers endured two trials, was publicly exposed as a former Communist and homosexual, and widely disbelieved in his accusations against Hiss, though the latter was finally convicted.

Chambers said afterward that the experience had made an old man of him. "It is three years," he wrote, "since I have been able to plow a field on this farm. I have sometimes thought that, if, in this coming spring, my son and I could simply work and seed a field and watch it sprout, an absolute healing would follow."[1]

Why would such a thing be so?

I think it's like this: Rejection is like water poured upon sand—it's impossible to keep from sinking in. You can fight against it, argue against it, label it unjust, but the fact remains that another human being or a society has rejected you.

You may have been at fault. You may have provoked the rejection somehow. But it doesn't help. To the contrary, it can make matters worse. Not only have you been rejected, but that judgment of you was to some degree justified.

You may find it hard to shake the feeling that you are a reject. You may wonder why you should go on living. Those who have rejected you have almost said that you shouldn't. They have written you off.

What you need is a strong word of acceptance—not from just anyone (though that would help), but from the One who counts most, from God. That's what you get when your own hands tend the soil. The seeds you plant will send up tender green shoots of new life as readily for you as for anyone else. This can be a token to you of God's love. Others have not obeyed his command to love you in spite of anything. But "He causes his sun to rise on the evil and the good, and sends rain on the righteous and the unrighteous" (see Matthew 5:43-48).

As you tend your plants day by day, you will sense that you and God are partners in this work. In Eden the first man was assigned this very activity—to dress and tend the garden. You are still God's creation, made in his image, object of his love and care.

The Animal Factor

Years ago a Christian leader known for his piety described what he recommended for people he judged were overstressed. "I tell them to go back home to the farm, wiggle their toes in the sand, and feed the chickens," he said.

That didn't sound like a very spiritual prescription to

me, but it did stick in my mind. And when I've needed it, I have found the principle very beneficial.

To those in extreme loneliness, the companionship of an animal can be virtually everything. Vera Figner spent many years alone in a prison cell. At length she befriended a little bird that flew to the barred window of her cell. The bird became tame enough to eat from her hand and to perch on her shoulder. It took up residence with her, became her cellmate. When it died, Vera wept for two weeks. She mourned that bird as we would mourn a loved one.

The Bible says, "All kinds of animals, birds, reptiles and creatures of the sea are being tamed and have been tamed by man" (James 3:7). Your potential choice of animal company is a wide one. Dogs and cats are favorites, of course, though some say cats are too aloof. One man said he preferred pigs because, "Dogs look up to you and cats look down on you, but pigs treat you as equals."

When you have been rejected, you need to be looked up to—so get a dog! The unqualified acceptance a dog offers can be affirming any time, no matter how successful or sophisticated you may be. The noted German theologian Helmut Thielicke writes concerning his pet dachshund, "I know that if something would happen to me, that your canine heart would be affected. You notice at once if something is bothering me. And if I am happy, then you make the most droll attempts to show me that you rejoice with me. . . . Our lives are more fully linked than I can say or you can bark."[2]

Getting the Strength to Reach Out

This "linking" of which Thielicke writes is exactly what a person needs who has become *unlinked* and lonely because of rejection. The linking process is precisely the means to reconnect an alienated person with others. Once we have reached out to a dog or other pet and made a friend, we are strengthened to reach out to the least threatening of our fellow humans in the same way. We realize there must be some people who are as good as dogs, people who will accept us, who will care about us, who will be enriched by our friendship.

We may want to begin with other "little" people, those society tends to neglect, such as the elderly, children, the poor. When we reach out to these people, we will be twice blessed because we help them and ourselves.

As for helping ourselves, becoming linked and staying linked to other people can actually save one's sanity. Samuel Johnson said, "Solitude is dangerous to reason, without being favorable to virtue." Vauvenargues probably expressed a better balance when he said, "Solitude is to the mind what fasting is to the body, fatal if it is too prolonged, and yet necessary." Both saw serious danger in too much solitude. Your own observation probably bears out the fact that people who are alone too much become odd.

The Christian, of course, is never really alone in the absolute sense. Our Lord not only stays with us but he indwells us. Nothing can separate us from him.

A Disappointed but Confident Apostle

One of the saddest passages of Scripture is also one of the most reassuring. It seems to me unspeakably sad that the apostle Paul should write, "At my first defense, no one came to my support, but everyone deserted me. May it not be held against them" (2 Timothy 4:16).

Here is a man who literally poured out his life and soul for others over many years. Thousands had come to know Christ through his ministry. He had blessed multitudes so that, if they could have done so, they would have plucked out their eyes and given them to him (see Galatians 4:14-15).

Now Paul is old. He is on trial for his life. The prospect of being thrown into an arena to be torn to shreds by a lion confronts him. And he is deserted.

"But the Lord stood at my side and gave me strength," Paul wrote (2 Timothy 4:17). The ever-present Christ! He is a companion and a remedy for loneliness in our greatest extremity.

We Need Each Other!

Still, it is not his plan that we have no companionship but his. Just as he indwells us, he also indwells every other true believer in the world. We are linked not only to Christ but to those who are Christ's. Whether they like it or not, and whether we like it or not, we are members one of another. We need to reflect that by involving ourselves with others.

Some of them may indeed try to say, "I don't need you." They are wrong. That is not the truth, and we must not reflect the same lie.

"The eye cannot say to the hand, 'I don't need you!' And the head cannot say to the feet, 'I don't need you!' On the contrary, those parts of the body that seem to be weaker are indispensable" (1 Corinthians 12:21-22).

We err when we count anyone as dispensable. Don't consider yourself superfluous, and don't dispense with others. The Lord of the church wants us all.

Relating to others is not just a nice idea. Brotherly kindness is a trait that Scripture commands us to add to our faith.[3] To develop this brotherly love may require that we defy a strong natural pull toward separation. Our every inclination may be to withdraw and nurse our private pain alone.

But to do so would be tragic. Choose brotherhood instead, for it leads to joy.

"How good and pleasant it is when brothers live together in unity!" (Psalm 133:1).

NOTES

1. Whittaker Chambers, *Witness* (New York: Random House, 1952), p. 799.

2. Helmut Thielicke, *Being a Christian When the Chips Are Down* (Philadelphia: Fortress Press, 1979), p. 70.

3. See Stanley C. Baldwin, *How to Build Your Christian Character* (Wheaton, Ill.: Victor Books, 1982) for a discussion of how to add goodness, knowledge, self-control, perseverance, godliness, brotherly kindness, and love to your faith.

Part 4

*Getting on
Top of It All*

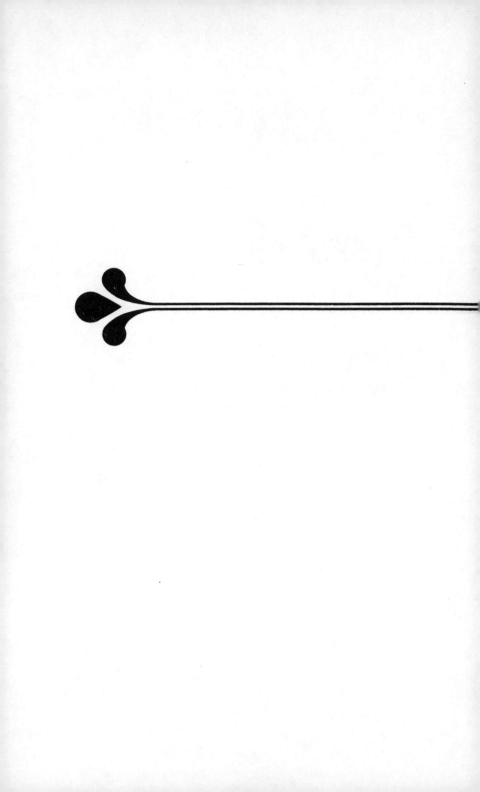

15
How to Celebrate No Matter What

When Disaster Strikes

What is one of the worst things that could possibly happen to you? Can you bring a specific calamity to mind? Think about it a minute. Now, what would you do if that actually happened? How would you handle it?

Perhaps you don't care much for my questions. You may not want to think about disaster. I can understand that, because I don't like to dwell on negative "what-ifs" either. On the other hand, I don't want to act like a frightened child who won't look under the bed because some menace might be lurking there. I don't want to be so threatened by life's darker possibilities that I can't even contemplate them.

But perhaps your situation is far different. Perhaps you don't need to imagine a "worst thing" happening. You are caught in some ordeal right now, and my asking how you would handle it seems ridiculous. As well talk about handling a tidal wave. Some things you don't handle; the challenge is sheerly to survive.

Believe me, I can understand that feeling, too. Yet I

am here to say that God can give us power to cope with anything that comes into our lives. Anything. In fact, we can do more than cope: We can celebrate!

Not that we can breeze through all our trials laughing, singing, and praising God. If that kind of life can be found anywhere, it's probably among the mentally ill. Such a life certainly cannot be found in the pages of the New Testament.

Jesus wept.

Peter endured enough suffering to write a book about it.

James counseled believers to pray about their afflictions and to endure them patiently.

Paul said it is through much tribulation that we must enter the kingdom, and he described himself as "troubled on every side." He further said that we should weep with those who weep—sharing the pain of others even when our own paths are pleasant (see Romans 12:15).

Nevertheless, as the Prison Epistles reveal, Paul not only had the strength to survive his trials but he also had the grace to rejoice despite his afflictions. He wrote, "Rejoice in the Lord always. I will say it again: Rejoice!" (Philippians 4:4).

Strength to go on and *grace to rejoice*—those are the qualities you and I need when things are tough.

Strength to Go On

Paul was a prisoner when he penned the words that have spoken strength to countless beleaguered Christians: "I can do everything through him who gives me strength" (Philippians 4:13).

I memorized those words as a teenager. I thought I understood them. My grasp of their implications, however, has been expanding ever since. Probably no passage has helped me more in tough times.

When I first became acquainted with Philippians 4:13, it was one of our youth group's memory verses. Even then I almost instinctively knew it was a misuse of the passage for Mary Beth to answer a question about her attendance at the Saturday night skating party by saying simply, "Philippians 4:13." To her it apparently meant she could wangle permission out of her reluctant parents.

Maybe she could. But was that how God intended us to understand and use the verse? I started thinking about it. If I didn't like Mary Beth's use of the verse, how should it be used?

"I can do all things . . ." I let my imagination take over, and it soon went to Superman. Did the verse mean I could leap tall buildings in a single bound? Could I stop a speeding train? Bounce bullets off my chest? Develop x-ray vision?

I decided Philippians 4:13 didn't mean I could literally do anything, no matter how fantastic.

Reading the context helped. Paul had evidently received a gift from the Christians at Philippi. He was glad to get it, but really more pleased with their giving than with his receiving. It showed grace and love on their part, and Paul rejoiced in that. So far as his needs were concerned, he could get along with or without their gift. He could handle being poor and deprived or being prosperous. He could "do all things" through Christ who strengthened him.

This put quite a different light on the verse. It wasn't talking about performing fantastic Superman exploits, but about being able to cope with material adversity or prosperity. To do that was no small accomplishment in itself. My buddy Bill Smith cited a passage from Proverbs that talked about the difficulty of doing that very thing.

> Give me neither poverty nor riches, but
> give me only my daily bread. Otherwise, I
> may have too much and disown you and

say "Who is the Lord?" Or I may become
poor and steal, and so dishonor the name
of my God (Proverbs 30:8-9).

Bill felt he was in the same boat with the writer of
Proverbs, and I had to admit I probably was, too. We
agreed that often people couldn't handle poverty and they
couldn't handle wealth, either. Through Christ, Paul
could do both.

While the verse sprang from a money context, however, it seemed to apply more broadly. No doubt the
Christ who strengthened Paul to handle want or plenty
also strengthened him to handle other tests in whatever
form they came. It seemed Paul was claiming to be an adequate person—equal to whatever might come in his life.
In other words, Paul knew how to cope no matter what.

That's why I asked you at the beginning of this chapter to contemplate the worst thing that could happen to
you and to think about how you would handle it.

The Testing Times

Most parents will likely identify with me when I say
that some of my own toughest times have come when my
children have been threatened. How I have needed the
strength of Christ to "do all things" then!

I vividly recall such an incident. I had reached a point
where I already had about all I could handle . . . and then
the *coup de grâce* fell.

My study load by itself had been heavy enough that
summer. Such strange-sounding subjects: Phonetics,
Phonemics, Morphology, Syntax. My wife Marge and I
were at the Summer Institute of Linguistics in Grand
Forks, North Dakota, taking our first tentative steps toward becoming missionary Bible translators.

We had left our infant son Steve back home in Oregon in care of an aunt and uncle. Kathy and Krystal, our

little sweetheart daughters aged three and two, were with us.

I was sick a lot that summer with a severe sore throat. At first I assumed it was "just a cold." But as it recurred with greater intensity and accompanying high fever, the sore throat became more and more puzzling and disturbing. I ended up in the infirmary for care and diagnostic tests.

"Have you ever had malaria?" our head nurse Trudy asked.

"No."

"Ever lived in the tropics, or even visited there?"

"No."

"Have you had scarlet fever?"

"No, but I was inoculated for it in Canada about three years ago, and ever since my left wrist has tended to sweat."

Trudy smiled. No, she didn't think that was significant.

Slowly the sore throat got better and I was released from the infirmary. A few days later it came time for our first in a series of inoculations required for Jungle Camp. Trudy gave us our shots one Saturday morning about nine o'clock. Marge then took Kathy with her for a trip into town, and I took Krystal with me for a brief stopover at the campus library.

I'd been at the library only a few minutes when I noticed Krystal was clenching her teeth and shivering. "Do you have to go potty?" I asked. She didn't reply but continued the strange behavior. I took her to the bathroom and sat her on the stool. She just sat there shaking, and it was obvious something was wrong.

But nothing to get very worried about, I thought. I knew where Trudy was; I'd just trot Krystal back over to her office and let her solve this little mystery.

I was hardly prepared for Trudy's reaction.

"Anaphylactic shock!" she cried out almost immediately. "She's having a reaction to the shots." In a flash Trudy was on the phone to the municipal hospital. "Anaphylactic shock," I heard her say. "We are bringing her in."

The seriousness of the situation still hadn't dawned on me. Our little sweetheart was the picture of health. Strong, happy, good-natured, a bit on the chubby side, she was the light of our lives. Kathy, our firstborn, was the classic beauty, but Krystal with her characteristic scowl at strangers and strange situations, her vulnerability, her complete trust in us, her goodness—Krystal had completely captured our hearts.

But now . . . in minutes she had been stricken, and I didn't grasp it yet. Whatever was wrong, it couldn't be serious. Wasn't Trudy right there to treat her as required? Even the quickly arranged trip to the hospital was reassuring. We'd have all the resources of medical science taking care of this little problem.

While enroute in the car, however, Trudy said something that let me know how things really were. "You'd better pray," she said. "Really pray. This reaction causes spasms—a sort of temporary paralysis. That's why her jaw's set. The spasms will pass, but . . . but meanwhile, if they reach her bronchial tubes, she wouldn't be able to breathe."

So I prayed. I begged God for the life of my little girl. And then, suddenly, a great weakness and weariness swept over me. I had borne the long, heavy studies. I had endured the protracted bout of sickness, from which I was still recovering. I had put up with this muggy, mosquito-infested place half a continent away from my home and my son. But to lose Krystal—that would be too much.

"I couldn't bear it, Lord," I cried. "You've got to save her!"

Then we were at the hospital. Krystal was quickly hooked to an intravenous apparatus. Marge arrived a few minutes later. She brought with her a little box of raisins—our usual treat for the girls—and something else very special, a Hershey bar. Krystal had tasted very little chocolate in her life, and how she loved it!

But now she lay so still and small in her bed that the raisins and the Hershey bar only served to emphasize how sick she was. The little eyes that would have glowed with delight were closed. The chubby fingers that would have dug to the bottom of the raisin box or clutched the chocolate so tightly lay curled and impassive.

Again I implored God to let her live.

He did. The crisis passed quickly and that evening we were able to take Krystal home. The next day she was as good as new. A few days later at a fellowship meeting, Trudy rose to say what an inspiration to her my patience in suffering had been. She knew—better than any of the others—what I had gone through with my own illness and with Krystal.

I was pleased, of course, but I knew something Trudy didn't. I knew I had been ready to break.

Learning to Cope

We never did become foreign missionaries (Krystal's reaction to the shots was only one of the reasons). I did serve as a pastor for some years, and then as a writer, editor, and speaker.

Twenty-seven years after the Grand Forks episode, I was scheduled to conduct a series of meetings for a large church in the Tri-Cities area of Washington state. Krystal had two little girls of her own by then and lived with her husband Bill and family in Moses Lake, Washington. We lived in the Portland area. Tri-Cities lay between the two, so the meeting gave us a great opportunity to get together.

One of the messages I planned to give was "How to Cope No Matter What." But could I cope, really, *no matter what?* Did I dare make such a claim? What if God let Satan put me to the test, like Job? What if he gave me a chance to prove I could cope? Did I want to risk provoking such a test?

I don't mean to suggest that I thought I was putting Krystal at risk, that he might test me again through her. No, any number of things could happen to me—things I couldn't even imagine. The Old Testament tells how God took away the reason of King Nebuchadnezzar to deal with his arrogance. The man went insane. The story concludes with a trenchant warning to all of us: "Those who walk in pride he is able to humble" (Daniel 4:37).

To suggest that I could cope no matter what *did* sound a bit arrogant. And yet there was Philippians 4:13: "I can do everything through him who gives me strength." Wasn't this Paul's testimony while he was in prison that he could cope no matter what?

So I preached it. I took Marge along for the meetings, Krystal and her family came down from Moses Lake, and we all had a marvelous time. The people received my message warmly. No calamity ensued to "teach me a lesson," and I felt sure I had "rightly divided" the Word.

Becoming Self-Sufficient

Some time later my friend John Wilkinson called and invited me to serve as devotional speaker at the annual men's Steelhead Fishing Retreat at Tapawingo in the Oregon Coast Range. "Talk to them about being *the adequate man,*" an inner voice said. I studied Philippians 4:13 and its context again to see if God would say something different to me or confirm what I had found before.

There was little question about it. Paul was claiming cope-ability. But wait. What was this other line in the context? "I have learned to be content whatever the circumstances" (v. 11).

Content? Did Paul mean he was perfectly satisfied to have it that way? Even when he was actually hungry and in want? His two self-descriptions seem almost contradictory. If you are *content,* you don't *want* anything. And if you are hungry, you are not content—at least not with your diet.

What did Paul mean by this word, *content?* How can the original be literally translated? "I for learned in what conditions I am self-sufficient to be." The word *content* literally means *self-sufficient.*

I dug out my Greek-English lexicon. The word in question is *autarkes,* and it occurs only once in Scripture— here, in Philippians 4:11. The prefix, *aut,* means *self.* Just like some familiar English words—*aut*omobile ("self-moving"), *auto*biography (a story about oneself). The *arkes* stem means *enough* or *sufficient.*

Paul wasn't saying that he was content; he was saying he had been made sufficient to handle whatever might come.

But why wasn't it translated that way? I checked several versions. Only one of them, the New American Standard Bible, introduced this *self-sufficient* idea, and then only in a marginal note. Why? Maybe I could guess . . . "I'm self-sufficient" sounds so arrogant! And I had thought my milder Tri-Cities message, "How to Cope No Matter What" might sound pompous.

Was it arrogance for Paul—and by extension for us— to claim total self-sufficiency? To make such a claim apart from the indwelling Christ certainly would be.

But we are not apart from Christ.

Never, under any circumstances, will he leave us or forsake us. I checked the Greek interlinear Bible for verse 13 and read, "All things can I do *in the one empowering me.*"

My mind went back to J. J. Ray, a salty Sunday school missionary I'd known years before. Praying at a formal church dedication, he shocked some of the crowd by saying, "Lord, I know you are here with us today, for I brought you with me when I came."

While one might have wished for a little more recognition of our corporate standing as the temple of God, J. J. was right. Christ actually indwells us who believe in him. How often Paul had said as much in the Prison Epistles! But I had missed it. Now I seemed to see it everywhere.

Paul prayed that we believers might know "the immeasurable greatness of his power *in us* who believe" (Ephesians 1:19, RSV).

He prayed that we might "be filled to the measure of all the fullness of God," and then immediately declared that God "is able to do immeasurably more than all we ask or imagine, according to his power that is *at work within us*" (Ephesians 3:19-20).

Paul wrote that this Christ-in-you concept was formerly a mystery—"hidden for ages and generations but is now . . . disclosed to the saints" (Colossians 1:26-27). The sad thing is that the reality of Christ in us is still hidden from many of the saints. We simply haven't grasped that we have God's *power* in us because we have *God* in us. That's the glorious message!

Designed for Power

Some time ago my son Steve brought me a Subaru station wagon to advertise and sell for him. I noticed that when I drove the thing, it was gutless. It could hardly make it up Mile Hill coming out to our place from town.

I didn't know if something was wrong with the car or if that was simply characteristic of Subarus. A friend called to ask that same question. "I just overhauled a Subaru," he said. "It seems to run okay now, but it's powerless. Is something wrong with it? Or is that normal for a Subaru?"

I still don't know whether Subarus are built for

power. But I do know about Christians. Believers can tap the limitless power of their Creator, and something is wrong if we lug down and barely make it up life's hills.

Paul was self-sufficient because he drew on the power of the indwelling Christ. He was a self-contained unit. He carried all the resources he needed right inside of him, and therefore he was equal to whatever came. That sufficiency is what we all have in Christ!

Grace to Rejoice

I have faced a few tough times since learning that I'm self-sufficient in Christ. The truth is I haven't always handled them with great ease.

I remember another difficult episode, another child, another hospital. Greg, our youngest, was eighteen when he crashed my motorcycle at highway speed into the side of a pickup truck that pulled in front of him. He could easily have been killed (and without a helmet probably would have been). As it was, he shattered his left knee, broke his wrist, and suffered many cuts and bruises.

Within a few days his knee had been surgically reconstructed and he was back home recuperating. We had all handled the trauma fairly well. But the worst was yet to come.

One week after the accident, Greg was seized with excruciating pain deep in his chest. It was about eleven P.M. Our urgent calls to the doctor brought reassuring words. "Probably just a muscle spasm, but bring him in."

Bring him in? Easily said, but it turned out to be almost impossible to do. Picture a big, strapping fellow more than six feet tall and weighing in excess of 180 pounds. His left leg is in a splint and he can hardly move for the pain. What do you do?

We had no choice but to call an ambulance out from town to our country home. Whoever dispatched the ambulance called our nearby fire department, too, and in moments emergency rescue arrived.

How reassuring! They got Greg on oxygen right away and were soon monitoring heart, blood pressure, and pulse. When the ambulance arrived, strong hands carried Greg on a stretcher to the vehicle's open doors. I rode along in the back with my son, while his mother followed in our car.

The attendant made radio contact with the emergency room, described Greg's vital signs, and communicated our estimated time of arrival. And then we were there.

A preliminary diagnosis indicated not a muscle spasm but a pulmonary embolism—a blot clot in the lungs. A clot had detached from somewhere in the body, probably the knee, and had lodged in the lung. Although this sometimes happens after surgery, it was rare, and especially in a patient so young.

The doctors administered anticoagulents to dissolve the clot and reduce the chance of more emboli. Greg would have to stay in the hospital at least a week. Because the anticoagulant would increase his risk of internal bleeding, even after he came home he would have to avoid riding in a car or doing anything that might cause injury. Otherwise he could bleed to death.

It was after two A.M. when Marge and I finally left the hospital and went home to bed. At five A.M. the phone rang. The nurse said Greg was asking for us.

When we reached his bedside, he had some hard questions. Why had all this happened to him? Was he such a terrible sinner? And why didn't God answer his prayers? He had prayed and prayed not to go through the pain and indignity of being catheterized again, as he had been during his previous hospitalization. His praying hadn't done any good.

I read to him from Hebrews 12. "Endure hardship as

discipline; God is treating you as sons. For what son is not disciplined by his father?" (v. 7). "God disciplines us for our good, that we may share in his holiness" (v. 10).

His mother talked to him about his relationship with the Lord. He had been going his own way and the Lord wanted him to change directions, to follow him.

After we talked awhile, Marge left the room. Greg had been given another pain pill and was trying to sleep. I sat there in a chair and listened to the words of the Scripture I had read as they reechoed in my mind. I didn't know how much or little the words had meant to Greg, but they surely hit home with me. "What son is not disciplined by his father?"

Greg had been our baby, eight years younger than his closest sibling, and he'd been spoiled. I'd gotten soft in my "old age." I'd never demanded enough from this kid, and now it was too late to do what I should have done earlier. Greg was legally of age and could pretty much do as he pleased.

If I hadn't disciplined him . . . God would.

My lack of sleep, the tension of Greg's illness, the spiritual struggle, my compassion for Greg's suffering— all this, combined with a sense of guilt, overcame me emotionally and I sat there in my chair and wept.

"I can do all things . . ."

"How to cope no matter what . . ."

"The adequate person . . ."

"Self-sufficient . . ."

I ask you: What kind of man sat there in that hospital room, weeping as gray dawn ushered in a new day (a Sunday, no less)? An adequate man? Or a broken one?

I can tell you it was really a man who, though needing an emotional release, was deep inside possessed of incredible strength. There's a difference, you see, between emotional/physical strength and spiritual strength. The former can be exhausted (and often is), but the latter comes in boundless supply. It is Christ in us, and not even our own guilt can drain that strength. Why? He indwells us by grace!

A Reason to Celebrate

We can celebrate that grace no matter what. Even if the worst happens and then that worst is twice compounded by our own behavior, we still have Christ within.

Always, whether at our best or our worst, we stand before him by grace. Always he indwells us. Always he is there to strengthen us.

I don't know any better reason to rejoice. Oh, it's great to rejoice when we've won. It's gratifying to know we've done well. We've met the tests, made the right choices, triumphed over our circumstances. But we don't always win, and we hardly ever score 100 percent. It is then that we can rejoice in God's grace. We can praise God that he doesn't desert us when we are down. He doesn't become a remote God—*up there* or *out there* somewhere, but no longer *here* in our hearts.

This is something we need to understand. In doing so, we are "strengthened . . . to have great endurance and patience." And we are lifted, "joyfully giving thanks to the Father" (Colossians 1:11-12).

Still Celebrating in Old Age

One of my most recent opportunities to preach the great truths about the indwelling Christ came at a Presbyterian church in Santa Clara, California. After the service, an elderly gentleman approached me and said, "I almost got up to interrupt you during your message." His unsmiling, intense manner made me think I was about to get blasted with scathing criticism.

"I am eighty-nine years old," he continued. "I discovered Philippians 4:13 only one year ago, and it has changed my life. When you were preaching I wanted to jump up and tell everyone, 'It's really true, folks!'"

I learned that this man had been a churchgoer most of his life, but was eighty-eight years old before he discovered the dynamic of Christ's power within him. He told me that all his life he had been a stammerer. He tried scores of remedies but nothing helped much.

That is, until he experienced the power of the indwelling Christ. His stammering disappeared.

"And guess what," he said excitedly, "I recently joined Toastmasters and I'm learning public speaking."

Isn't that great? Ah, to be celebrating life at age eighty-nine. That's for me!

Still, I must confess that there are times even now when I don't cope well. They come when I forget the strength and power available to me. It's easy to get your eyes so fixed on the problem that you can't see your inner resources.

Peter knew that. Even after walking on water, he began to sink when he focused on the howling wind and the foaming waves around him.

At such times, however, it takes only a word from Jesus to lift us above the circumstances once again. That word so many times has come from Philippians 4:13.

Paul could do all things through Christ.

I, too, can do all things through Christ.

An eighty-nine-year-old former stammerer in Santa Clara can do all things through Christ.

What about you?

A NOTE TO THE READER

This book was selected by the same editors who prepare *Guideposts*, a monthly magazine filled with true stories of people's adventures in faith.

If you have found inspiration in this book, we think you'll find monthly help and inspiration in the exciting stories that appear in our magazine.

Guideposts is not sold on the newsstand. It's available by subscription only. And subscribing is easy. All you have to do is write Guideposts Associates, Inc., Carmel, New York 10512. A year's subscription costs only $7.95 in the United States, $9.95 in Canada and overseas.

When you subscribe, each month you can count on receiving exciting new evidence of God's presence and His abiding love for His people.